DARIO SPEEDWAGON

DARIO
SPEEDWAGON

Rise of the Champion

Neil Drysdale

BIRLINN

This edition first published in 2008 by
Birlinn Limited
West Newington House
10 Newington Road
Edinburgh
EH9 1QS

www.birlinn.co.uk

ISBN – 978 1 84158 763 9

British Library Cataloguing-in-Publication Data
A catalogue record for this book is available from the British Library

Typeset in Sabon by Palimpsest Book Production Limited,
Grangemouth, Stirlingshire

Printed and bound by
Clays Ltd, St Ives plc

CONTENTS

ACKNOWLEDGEMENTS

I would like to thank a significant number of people for their valuable assistance and insight while helping me write this book. Dario Franchitti himself has been a source of inspiration to me ever since I first started covering his exploits when his little racing car was parked in Whitburn, West Lothian, and long before he had headed off to the United States. Dario is one of the most modest, level-headed and genial individuals it would be possible to encounter in a sport which is so often dominated by giant-sized egos and/or rampant narcissism, so meeting and speaking to Dario on a regular basis, all the way through from his emergence as a talented teenager to winning the Indy 500 in the fabled Brickyard, has been one of the best experiences of my journalistic career.

Secondly, I would like to acknowledge the help and expertise which has been provided by Sir Jackie Stewart, possibly the greatest living sporting Scot, and a fellow who has always made time to offer me his views and share his passionate recollections of his time in and around motor-sport. One of the most galling aspects of the wretched Max Mosley's survival as president of FIA, motor-sport's governing body, in 2008 was the fact that too few people seem to have remembered his disgraceful personal attack on Sir Jackie in 2007, in which he labelled the three-times world champion as a 'certified halfwit'. Not only is this palpably untrue, but in terms of decency, sporting excellence and the inspirational qualities which have surrounded his remarkable life, Jackie is ten times the man Mosley will ever be.

There are many others who have furnished me with information, for which I am very appreciative. Some did not wish to be named, and I have respected their wishes, but the others include: Nigel Clyde, Martyn Pass, Marcus Simmons, Marc Orme, Jeremy Shaw, Mike Brudenell, Stewart Roden, Ed Wallace, Bill MacDonald and Stevie Murray. I would also like to record my gratitude for the insights which the late David Leslie provided me with about Dario's early career, before his premature death in tragic circumstances earlier this year. This, sadly, is something of a theme in these pages.

Thanks are also due to Neville Moir, Andrew Simmons and Peter Burns at Birlinn and my agent, Mark Stanton. And finally, when my desk-top computer suffered irretrievable damage in June, I could not have kept a grip on this project without the assistance and encouragement of my wife, Dianne. Ironic, perhaps, that a book which chronicles the life of a man at the forefront of cutting-edge technology should be written by a Luddite!

1

DIFFERENT WORLDS

It's approaching one o'clock on a late March afternoon in 2008 and an implacable swirl of snow is starting to spread a white blanket over Bathgate. Outside the local bakers, a queue has formed, with the hot-pie-and-bridie collective awaiting their daily rations, oblivious to the efforts of the Scottish Government to persuade the population to alter its eating habits. Indeed, walking up the tawdry pedestrian precinct, there was the unmistakable sense of a once-vibrant community in gradual decline, characterised by the litany of charity shops, 'Supersavers'-style emporia and graffiti-smeared flowerpots, which look almost as incongruous as Katie Price in a nunnery.

Even when George Clooney's production company visited this hub of West Lothian in 2004, to shoot scenes for his film *The Jacket*, the comparison between the American auteur's massive wealth and the rows of threadbare food outlets and pubs, struggling along on a regimen of unhappy hours for doleful souls, was painfully obvious. The implementation of the smoking ban at least made the task of conducting vox pops easy, although the sight of grey old men, possibly in their mid-50s, clutching at their gaspers as though they were a distillation of ambrosia and nectar, rather dampened the occasion. But, none the less, I persevered in asking a cross-section of the citizenry, huddled under the awnings and makeshift smoke shelters, whether they were aware of the thriving motor-sport dynasty resident in their town, and their responses ranged from the couldn't-care-less to the borderline psychotic. Eventually, one shaven-haired monobrow sneered at my inquiry and replied menacingly: 'Are you taking the piss? Are you? Well, if you know where there is a Ferrari or a BMW hidden in this dump, why don't you jump into it, ya dobber, and f***ing well leave the rest of us alone to enjoy our fags.'

As should quickly have become obvious, any resemblance shared by Bathgate with Hollywood is purely coincidental, yet if one peeks beneath the surface, the link between a fading relic of the coal mining and British Leyland era and the trappings of Tinseltown fame assert themselves in the remarkable career of Dario Franchitti, one of those blithe individuals for whom travel has broadened the mind as well as building him up into a more recognisable face in New York and Nashville than he is in his homeland.

Nowadays, if Dario can stroll down Glasgow's Sauchiehall Street or Edinburgh's Royal Mile without eliciting a second glance, it is a price he will gladly pay. After all, he grew up in West Lothian, in the bosom of a family who were relentlessly obsessed with motoring, machinery and the minutiae of what makes things tick, without ever blowing his own trumpet, and although life in the fast lane can often be a milieu for pampered egotists with raging libidos and excessive self-esteem, Franchitti remains wedded to his roots. He may have swept to a magnificent victory in the Indy 500 classic race in 2007, and subsequently driven to the overall Indy Racing League championship in the most dramatic of circumstances, but he is still the same charming fellow, who seamlessly makes the transition between attending Oscar ceremonies and satisfying the paparazzi, in the company of his actress wife, Ashley Judd, and visiting Parkhead, whenever he can grasp an opportunity to watch his beloved Celtic, with his mates from the past.

As somebody who has known Franchitti since he was a teenager, and who has interviewed him on a regular basis, I can confirm that he is a plum subject for gentle interrogation. In one instance, when he strolled into the offices of *Scotland on Sunday* back in 2001, clad in denims and an Italian football top, several of the canteen staff asked me, their tongues almost hitting the ground, whether they could have his autograph. The photographs were soon signed, along with a few cracks from Dario about the quality of the croissants and pastries on sale, and there was no trace of hubris or the 'Look at me' prima donna-ism which is the bane of so many of his counterparts. Instead, Franchitti grew up with his priorities in the right place. Family came first and friends thereafter, with sport as the third element in the equation. This has been clear whenever close comrades have – regrettably too frequently – perished on the race track, as did his Canadian contemporary, Greg Moore, in 1999, or when his compatriot, Colin McRae, was killed in a helicopter crash, which also claimed the lives of three others, including two small boys, in 2007. In what had proved to be the season that Franchitti enjoyed unprecedented success, he would have been entitled to concentrate on the positives in his end-of-term report. But, typically, he recognised that any sporting achievement was rendered all but immaterial by comparison with the death of four people – McRae and his five-year-old son, Johnny; family friend, Graeme Duncan, and six-year-old Ben Porcelli – in a tragic accident and he spoke movingly, after attending the funerals, of the impact of the dreadful event.

'That's the thing: as good as the rest of 2007 might have

been for me, I will always regard it as the year that we lost Colin and Johnny,' said Franchitti, the quiver in his voice reflecting his distress. 'Colin was two things – he was a hero to people all across the world, but he was also my pal – we had done so many good things together – and it is terrible to realise that he has gone.' There was a pause and he strove for a few seconds to gather his thoughts, but the message was clear: whether or not kind words made any difference to the grieving McRae family, he would be offering prayers for them all.

This is the fashion in which Franchitti has lived his life ever since he first came into the world in 1973. For what has seemed like an eternity, he has flirted with triumph on the IndyCar and IRL circuits, whilst experiencing a litany of woes, whether falling off his motorbike and sustaining serious injury on a trip home to West Lothian, or being left stymied and seething with silent frustration through suffering mechanical failure or the unsought intervention of the fates in dashing his aspirations. But, despite the setbacks, and irrespective of myriad ghosts and gremlins in the machine, he is essentially the same individual now that he was back in the 1980s and 1990s. Straight from the outset, he has always possessed an uncommon mixture of hard-nosed realism and spirit of adventure, treating the mundane and the memorable with equal attention.

As a teenager, I once asked him what had attracted him to motor sport and his reply epitomised rare maturity. 'To be honest, I have never known a time when I wasn't fascinated by speed and by going as fast as I could, and I suppose it was in the genes. Both my grandfathers were incredibly interested in cars and the torch was passed down from one generation to another, to the stage where you can't really imagine life without being involved with motors and watching Formula One on television and going to karting circuits . . . basically, becoming steeped in the whole business, so that no one part of it is any different from the other. My father, George, raced go-karts and little cars at Ingliston. As soon as I saw these vehicles, I was entranced by them, and I have this memory of saying to my parents: "Can I do that?" I had a go-kart when I was three, with a tiny Honda engine on the back, and I was as pleased as I could ever have been.'

In those early days, the name Franchitti was best-known around Whitburn and Bathgate as a purveyor of ice cream, cigarettes and carbonated drinks, whilst the family connection with another Scots-Italian clan, the Di Restas, has produced a veritable string of motoring connections. First, there was George Franchitti, spending his weekends wherever there was racing action, either competing or spectating at circuits such as Larkhall in the west of Scotland, Ingliston, near Edinburgh and the home for the annual Royal Highland Show, and Knockhill in Fife. One contemporary of the bold George described him as 'fast, but occasionally too inclined to be reckless'. Another recalls him as 'an out-and-out flier, who clearly enjoyed pushing the throttle, but was more interested in speed than reliability or even moving in a straight line'. Dario, for his part, caught the bug immediately, not just from watching his father, but also from the example of his uncle, Louis Di Resta, who was 13 years his senior, but still capable of serving up high-octane thrills and adrenaline-laced excitement, albeit with a seriously aggressive edge.

Yet if they were mustard-keen to prove their worth, that quality was a necessity for anybody growing up in West Lothian in the late 1970s. Whitburn was a dreich, featureless community, with Polkemmet Colliery, British Leyland and the Levi's jeans factory providing the majority of jobs for those in employment. Normal day-to-day existence revolved around grimy hard labour and prosaic industry.

There were occasional flickerings of escape for the population – the annual Gala Day offered children enough E numbers
to turn them into Zebedee and a greater amount of Irn-Bru
and Red Kola than was good for their digestive systems,
before the town's more athletic youngsters participated in the
various sprint races at the King George V Park. For the adults,
there was the procession, featuring a variety of decorative
floats, and a parade of flute, silver and brass bands, to be
enjoyed/endured (depending on one's tolerance levels), as the
prelude to the menfolk flooding into the Double Five, the
Cross Tavern, the Clachan and the Miners' Welfare Club,
where, three or four sheets to the wind in mid-afternoon, they
would be heard to exclaim: 'Och aye, it's a grand day for
the kids, isn't it?' On these afternoons, it was easy to imagine
that life would continue in its present form ad infinitum, but
Margaret Thatcher and Arthur Scargill changed all that.
Indeed, by the middle of the 1980s, Polkemmet had closed
down, Leyland suffered a similar fate, and unemployment
was rampant in every age group. Whitburn's main thorough-
fare, West Main Street, reflected the transformation. Short-lived
shops opened and closed, specialising in Venetian blinds,
tanning products, technological innovations (most notably,
giant mobile phones and ghetto blasters which were as cheap
as they were impractical) and, for those of us who departed
to Edinburgh or London and only occasionally returned, it
seemed that just about the only permanent features of the
Whitburn retail scene were the Di Restas' café and Franchitti's
ice-cream parlour.

In those days, the infamous mantra from Westminster
was: 'On your bike.' But for Dario and the other young
aces who emerged from the 1970s, both inspiring each
other and receiving assistance from wise aficionados of
the motoring business behind the scenes, the passage to
prominence arrived via karts. Franchitti came into the world

two years after David Coulthard and three after Allan McNish, but although the triumvirate hailed from different areas of Scotland – the latter duo were born in Twynholm and Dumfries respectively – their paths crossed quickly, repeatedly and with such a recurring rhythm that even as youngsters, there were indications in their psychological make-up and instinctive ease in handling machinery which hinted at greatness in store. Three decades later, they all have fabulous riches, property in Monaco, a sprawling state-of-the-art collection of Boys Toys, and a collective CV studded with honours and triumphs in such illustrious events as the British Grand Prix (Coulthard), Le Mans (McNish) and the Indy 500 (Franchitti). But, long before these challenges had been laid before the Scots, these beetle-browed fellows were nurtured, encouraged and cajoled by the kind of stalwart figures whose accomplishments are undiminished by their relative anonymity.

David Leslie, for instance, was never happier than when absorbed in the twin tasks of pushing himself and his vehicles to the limit, and avoided straying into solipsistic indulgence when he could pass on advice to those in his slipstream. A national karting champion five times before he won the Formula Ford title in 1978, Leslie, the son of a passionate motor-sport crusader of the same name, subsequently moved into touring cars and formed an allegiance with the Ecurie Ecosse team, whilst recording a string of creditable across-the-range performances for such disparate organisations as Aston Martin, Silk Cut Jaguar and Team Marcos.

Yet, if he was a fiercely competitive individual behind the wheel, Leslie was also a seasoned dispenser of crucial life lessons for the next generation, in the mould of Franchitti, in whom he recognised a youngster with a rare natural talent, as he explained to me, during a conversation in 1998. 'The thing about Dario, from almost the first time I met him, was the look in his eyes when he started talking about his goals, his ambitions, and his fascination with cars, with what made them tick, and never being content with making up the numbers if there was anything he could do to bridge the gap and chase his dreams. You meet a lot of youngsters around the karting circuit who are enthusiastic and have ability, but the best ones have something extra, something which you can't really express in words, but which gives them an advantage, and Dario was always focused on how he could get better. He wanted to learn, he asked question after question, and he soaked up the knowledge from all those around about him. A lot of the other teenagers were pretty much as you would expect: they wanted to be cool, or tough, or a mixture of the two, and the majority of them fell by the wayside soon enough. But Dario knew that his parents were making sacrifices to allow him to pursue his dream and, straight from the outset, he wasn't interested in anything else but the quest for self-improvement. It was as if he had decided from 11 or 12 that this was going to be his life and that he had better take it as seriously as he would if he had been committed to any other career choice.'

These qualities convinced Leslie that his compatriot was destined for fame, even if there was no fortune at the outset. On the contrary, Franchitti may have been affluent in terms of the average West Lothian resident – and, for those of us who patronised his family's shops, the contrast between entering these stores and witnessing a cornucopia of exotic confections and the residual drabness of the rest of the Whitburn retail community illustrated the latter's ongoing struggle with penury – but he and his father travelled thousands of miles together to a variety of circuits across Britain, often existing on motorway service-station stodge and an unshakeable belief in what they were doing. Even when Dario heard of David Leslie's death in yet another air accident – in

Kent at the end of January 2008 – his sadness was tinged with a heartfelt appreciation for the close-knit nature of the Scottish motoring community, and gratitude for the fashion in which men such as Leslie had eased his development and refined his skills.

'It's just so bloody sad. I was thinking about David all the way home from (the NASCAR) race at Martinsville. There were two sides to him, David the racer and David the team owner, and my dad would always rave about David's driving in karting and Formula Ford and how he went on to have great success with Ecurie Ecosse and its wee Group C car and then on the next step up into touring cars. I got to see him race when he was in tin tops and I was driving for his team in the Vauxhall junior, and then when I was in Vauxhall Lotus and Formula 3 as well. He was bloody amazing, especially in that Ecurie Ecosse Vauxhall Cavalier. To see him take on the works boys, who had far bigger resources at their disposal, and beat them was fantastic to watch.

'The other side of him, the one I really knew, was in his capacity as a team boss. You have got to mention his father too and his role in making the equation work. They were a real team and each brought their own area of expertise to the table. They wanted the young Scottish drivers to have the advantages they didn't have when David was coming up through the ranks in the early 1970s. They had done a terrific job with Allan [McNish] and DC [David Coulthard] so it was only natural that I would go with them too, and although it was tough for us to find the money at first, the pair of them were so understanding and so dedicated to the cause that nothing seemed to faze them.

'David had an amazing way of explaining things and I can still picture him in my mind's eye doing it: he would stand with his legs slightly apart, hunch over a wee bit, hands shoulder-width apart, and he would start to explain how to do something through the corner. He had a knack for putting his message across in such a way that you never forgot it. He would talk you through it, step by step, patiently, almost hypnotically, and you would think: 'Okay, the penny has dropped' and you just went out and did it. The bottom line was that he loved the sport and he would spend hours talking to anybody who cared about it or was even slightly interested in it. Once he started chatting at the Scottish Motor Racing Dinner every year, he was captivating company and we will all really miss him. A few of us are lucky enough to gain opportunities to go out into the world and take part in some of the biggest events in international sport. But we wouldn't be able to do that without the influence and the encouragement of people like David Leslie.'

Franchitti's tribute reflects his family values and unwavering belief in communal ties. Even now, when he is married to a Hollywood actress, and when he has transcended the slightly-frustrating experience of being known as 'Ashley's husband' by generating his own headlines, he regularly journeys back to Scotland for reunions with the same friends he made on his ascent to prominence. There are no airs, requests for pampered treatment, nor recourse to the insufferable outburst 'Do you know who I am?' which once landed a world-famous tennis star in hot water when a gallus check-in worker called his bluff by announcing over the tannoy: 'Could I have some help at gate 13? There's a gentleman here who doesn't know who he is!' West Lothian, in general, is no place for the faint-hearted, nor the affected, but it can deal with swollen egos and over-inflated reputations, much as the old miners from Polkemmet would react to trouble at the pit. 'Growing up in Bathgate and Whitburn makes you grounded and aware that you are living in the real world,' Dario told me, early on in his career, even as he spoke about the manner in which his great-great-grandparents had originally made their way from Italy to Scotland, and how he was proud of his dual links. 'Some people have asked me about my helmet, which features both the Scottish saltire and the Italian tricolour, but I just tell them that I have a connection to both countries and perhaps that has moulded me into the person I am. When I was very little, I remember looking at the cars in one of my dad's motoring magazines, and I was hooked on how fantastic the Ferraris were, but I also started reading about Jim Clark and soon appreciated that he was one of the best motor racing drivers who has ever lived. Both the Scots and the Italians love Formula One, and when you look back at the great names, many of them come from the two nations, so I think I am fortunate to have an affinity with both. Certainly, wherever I go in the United States, most folks have heard of Jim Clark and Jackie Stewart and everybody knows what a Ferrari car looks like, so these names have stamped themselves on the world.'

It might be overly glib to attribute Franchitti's renown to a frost-and-fire combination of Scottish pragmatism and Italian pizazz, but he has straddled the challenge of dwelling in parallel universes with a striking success. Back in 1990, when we first met, he invited me for a chat at Di Resta's café, on East Main Street, an establishment which served a wondrous hamburger'n'onions with a to-die-for aroma, and some of the creamiest, most tempting coffee it is possible to imagine (certainly finer than anything on offer at the plethora of present day franchised establishments). He was only 17, but by that stage, Franchitti had already won the Scottish Junior Karting Championship in 1984, the British equivalent two years later, and the senior titles in 1988. He was attracting attention from both petrolheads and the sort of ephemeral sporting fans who become avid followers of tennis for a fortnight at Wimbledon every year and golf for eight days at the US Masters in April and the Open championship in July.

In which light, and considering that Franchitti had found himself behind a wheel before he did a school desk, it might have been understandable if he had been either blasé, or star-struck, or inclined to preen in the spotlight. Yet, as it transpired, he was modest, reticent about making any grand claims for himself, and immediately apologised for the fashion in which my photographer companion and myself had been chased on our arrival by a giant canine creature which made the Hound of the Baskervilles resemble Eddie from *Frasier*. Revelations were forthcoming, but they were delivered in a soft lilt, albeit with the compressed excitement of somebody who could scarcely believe they were being paid to climb into a racing vehicle five days week. 'It has been a terrific experience so far. The foundation came from going to the West of Scotland Karting Club in Larkhall and the competition there was ferocious, but so was the amount of support I received, before heading down to England and into Europe to keep aiming higher and higher.'

Franchitti had only recently begun the graduation process into the rigorous – and expensive – domain of Formula 3. 'David Coulthard and Allan McNish had gone to race with David Leslie and his dad, who were running a successful team and they put together a deal for me to race before the season started. But it wasn't easy, and I have my parents to thank for being able to step up. They remortgaged the house to allow me to do that, and you don't do these things lightly.'

His memories were as diverse as one might expect from a peripatetic individual but even as a teenager his attitude was: that he would venture where the action was, seek out would-be sponsors, learn to cope with the often absurd demands of the media, and turn himself into a package, without relinquishing his own idiosyncratic traits. 'Most of my life has been spent in West Lothian, and sometimes when I say to people I want to be a racing driver, they look at me as if I am living on a different planet. It's like, if you come from this area, you shouldn't have that kind of ambition. But when you study a bit of the history of what Jim [Clark] and Jackie Stewart achieved, and when you go to the circuits at Larkhall or Ingliston or further north in Scotland, you soon realise how many thousands of fans and dedicated souls there are out there. Of course it can sometimes get a bit daunting and I am trying to take one step at a time. Equipment is expensive. Safety is expensive. Travel costs stack up over the course of a month, let alone a year and I have already been involved in this sport for more than a decade. In racing, even from the first level, you spend tens of thousands of pounds a year and that still offers no guarantee of success. But if it was supposed to be easy, then I guess it wouldn't be much of a challenge, would it?'

That interview was significant if for no other reason than that it signalled Franchitti's inclusion in a *Scotland on Sunday* list of talented youngsters to watch out for in the 1990s. Such enterprises are invariably fraught with hazards: for every promising mini-star with lofty aspirations, there are a dozen hard-luck stories, and a hundred reasons why adolescent potential remains unfulfilled. Yet, in Franchitti's case – and that of another of our choices, John Higgins from Wishaw, who subsequently became the world snooker champion – there was sufficient maturity and tough-as-teak realism to indicate that these characters would not be fazed by temporary blips in form or financial glitches.

By the stage we next met – in 1992 – Dario had won the prestigious McLaren/Autosport Young Driver of the Year award, a prize which frequently precedes global recognition, as evidenced by its list of winners including Coulthard, Jenson Button and Lewis Hamilton. Yet, once again,

Franchitti showed no sign of wanting to toot his own horn, spelling out instead how he was developing a growing fascination with two of Scotland's most significant sporting dramas: the life and death of Jim Clark and the unprecedented achievement of Celtic's footballers in becoming the first British club to lift the European Cup with a momentous victory over Inter Milan on a merry May day in 1967.

'What the Celtic guys did was proof that you don't have to spend hundreds of millions of pounds to build a team with skill and passion and who are playing for each other, every single moment of every single match,' said Franchitti, on the eve of an explosion of inflation-busting transfers in the one-time beautiful game. 'I have heard about the Celtic players from my dad and it is incredible that the whole of the European Cup-winning side should have come from such a small area (within a 15-mile radius), but it shows what can be done and how Scots don't have to feel inferior to anybody in the world of sport.

'As for Jim, I have spoken to Jackie Stewart and David Leslie, senior and junior, about his abilities and soaked up what they have told me, but watching the tapes of his races blows me away. He was incredible, just incredible. To be in such control of the car as he was in winning world titles and to go to the Indy 500 and win that as well [in 1965] demonstrated that he could do anything he desired, and with such humility. All Scots should be proud of Jim Clark, because he epitomised the best of what we can be. If any of the rest of us ever get close to what he did, I can tell you we will be going some.'

For the next 15 years, Dario and I kept in touch, as he chased down his goals, largely from within the United States. Occasionally, the chats would become slightly awkward, because the more he strove to attain titles, the greater the variety of obstacles seemed to lie in wait. One sensed that he might have fancied a move to Formula One, but Franchitti was admirably insistent that he had no wish to join Bernie Ecclestone's circus for money alone if his fate thereafter was to sit 14th or 15th on the starting grid every fortnight. Off the track, nobody could possibly have quibbled with his sharp business acumen or doubted his happiness after marrying Ashley Judd, the star of such cinematic offerings as *Kiss the Girls, Double Jeopardy, Heat* and *High Crimes* and a woman described as 'an intellectual pin-up' by her own mother, Naomi. However, there remained a feeling of talent denied full expression. On a superficial level, he was in a young man's dreamland: when he wasn't negotiating oval circuits at 220mph, he was water-skiing on Scottish lochs, flying his helicopter or, with his gears at full throttle, zooming into the distance on his £18,000 Augusta motorbike. As a (more cynical) colleague once remarked to me: 'Hasn't done badly for a failure, has he!' And yet . . . there were tragedies, too, including the death of his confrère, Moore, in 1999, as well as his involvement in a 150mph bike crash which could have snapped the lid on his existence, let alone his career, in the spring of 2003.

Franchitti appreciates the dangers inherent in his vocation as much as anyone. On YouTube, there is video footage of several of his battles with gravity which look as if they are CGI-enhanced snapshots from a Tarantino movie. Yet, befitting his reputation as a steely competitor with a survivalist's mentality, he fields questions on life and death with the meticulous assuredness which embodies his driving. On the night when he was pipped to the CART title by Juan Pablo Montoya in 1999, the tussle was overshadowed by the demise of Moore, who perished in a truly ghastly accident, but Franchitti dealt with the subject in a no-nonsense manner. 'Naturally, what happened to Greg was dreadful at the time, and I felt horrible about the whole thing, but you have to climb back onto the car and push yourself to the maximum, because otherwise there is no point carrying on, and I think we all accept that there are risks when we sign on the dotted line. Am I scared about crashing? Do I think about death? Well, I believe that any driver who comes out and says that they don't is lying, but you can't afford to dwell excessively on the subject. No, it is how you react to the possibility which is important and, equally, you should concentrate on the positive aspects of our sport. There's the adrenaline rush when you are moving at 230mph, the buzz of overtaking an opponent, the giddy feeling of pushing yourself to the limit and the sensation when everything comes together in one race and you go out and take the checkered flag and then gaze at the faces of your team members when you get back into the pits and realise you've nailed it.'

Privately, Franchitti must have wondered whether he was ever destined to savour that ecstasy in the build-up to the 2007 Indy 500, one of the most fabled races on the motoring calendar, and an extravaganza which Dario himself described to me as his profession's Oscars or Superbowl: one of those rare instances where Stateside families sit down together and find themselves enraptured by something quintessentially American. When his challenge faltered in 2005, on the 40th anniversary of his compatriot Clark's win, Franchitti was uncharacteristically off-colour in public, saying baldly: 'I'm pissed about that.' However, if whatever could have gone wrong did so, matters were remedied spectacularly amidst the pandemonium and chaos which surrounded the 2007 vintage, where the Scot, benefiting as he later admitted from a combination of the weather and his own good fortune, emerged from left-field to seize the cherished prize. And, better still, he did so in scenes which might have been lifted from a Hollywood movie.

On that Sunday evening, while the rest of his Andretti

Green racing team were uncorking bottles of champagne, hollering paeans to 'The Speedwagon' and hyperventilating with high fives, Dario and his wife slipped away from the throng and raised their glasses in toasting an achievement which they feared might never materialise. 'My husband is a gifted man and I told him: "Babe, just pick the others off",' said Judd, a fragrant presence with a nose for news and an eye for the main quote. 'He raced from 14th to first, ignored the rain, and any other distractions and I am oh-so very proud of him. This is so overdue for him.' Franchitti, for his part, sipped a mineral water, even as he paid homage to his hero, the iconoclastic Clark. 'We are restoring an old house in Scotland and we have created a room which is dedicated to Jim. I have a scale model of the vehicle he drove when he triumphed at this circuit, all those years ago, and to think that I should have followed in his footsteps is a dream come true, even if it hasn't really sunk in yet.'

By the following morning, the scale of Franchitti's exploits was beginning to register, even as the American media flocked to the Indianapolis Motor Speedway. Ever since Dario (whose name was spelt out phonetically – 'DAH-ree-oh Fran-KEE-tee – in many publications) and Ashley tied the knot at Skibo Castle in Scotland, they had become as instantly recognisable throughout the United States on red carpets and at film premieres as David and Victoria Beckham were in Blighty, and although the couple could saunter down most main streets in this country without garnering the paparazzi's attention, they had settled comfortably into A-list status during the previous five years. The principal difference between them and the Beckhams was that they had no interest in publicity stunts (and we could add that both are talented in their own spheres), which explained why a global audience responded so affectionately to the good vibrations which resonated between the Franchittis in the aftermath of victory. The actress had turned up at the Brickyard on Sunday, without any fanfares or minders, and stood quietly, unobtrusively, with the other 350,000 fans. When she finally realised he was the champion, she ran to Victory Lane, lifted her face to the sky, kissed Franchitti, and hugged him for several minutes, before escorting him to the post-race press conference, where she refused interview requests with the simple explanation: 'This isn't about me. This is about my man.'

Obviously, neither was overly concerned about the $1.6m which Franchitti's triumph earned him. Their combined wealth had been estimated at £200m, they owned a lavish home in Nashville, Tennessee, as well as other properties in Britain and Europe, and boasted a string of friends within the film and F1 empire – the pair had been photographed, at various times, with such luminaries as George Clooney, Brad Pitt, Sylvester Stallone, Sharon Stone, Morgan Freeman, Al Pacino and Michael Schumacher. But, none the less, until Franchitti bounded out from the pack to reign supreme in the rain, in the 91st running of the Indy 500, there was a widespread conviction that the Scottish driver would be remembered as a good, not great, sporting competitor.

There were also murmurings that he should have thrown his hat into the Grand Prix ring, oblivious to Franchitti's protestations that he was happier challenging for honours than making up the numbers. 'Everybody talked about F1 this and F1 that, and I was linked with various teams for a lengthy period, but F1 didn't have any appeal unless I was in a car with a chance of pushing for the title and the opportunity never arose. To be honest, I have always reckoned that the championships over here in America are more open, in any case – every weekend, you have eight or nine different people with a serious chance of winning, be it in the Indy Racing League, or Champ Cars, or NASCAR. What's done is done, and I am not one for regrets or thoughts on what might have been. Why should I when I have just realised one of the biggest ambitions in my life?'

It was a salutary recognition of the man, his methodology and guiding philosophy in his domain, that the rest of the IRL drivers paid their respects, not with half-hearted platitudes, but the warm endorsements of men who were genuinely pleased for the limey in their midst. 'When he first arrived in the States,' said one American motoring journalist, 'nobody could fathom how a guy with such an Italian name could have such a Scottish burr, but we soon found out that his grandfather [Albert, a restaurateur and one of life's gentlemen] had migrated from Italy to Scotland and pretty soon, especially once he married Ashley, the crowds took him to their hearts. Finally now, Dario will be acclaimed as the winner of the 2007 Indy 500 and not just as Ashley Judd's other half. And everyone is happy for him, because of the kind of guy he is. Beloved. Appreciated. Felt for.'

The words propelled me back to a conversation I had entered into with a US magazine writer on the eve of Franchitti's wedding. This particular woman seemed fascinated by ice cream, sliders, cones and 99s, to such an extent that one wondered if she was on a retainer from Ben 'n' Jerry, but she also asked an interminable litany of questions about Whitburn, and about brass bands (the town's ensemble are regular national champions), barber shops (they do a fine line in tonsorial variations on a theme) and bigotry (still, regrettably, a pervasive influence, explaining why several Protestants once refused to attend the opera company's production of *Finian's Rainbow*). All of this suggested that she was operating from the Bumper Book of Killer B subjects and was less concerned with control panels than controversy. Mercifully, though, as I related my recollections of the exemplary manner in which Dario had dragged himself up from karts and diminutive automobiles towards the pinnacle of the fast lane, she sounded increasingly crest-fallen. 'But surely, the guy has to have some skeletons in his closet,' she asked desperately. 'I mean, nobody's perfect. And yet I can't find a bad word about him. What gives?'

'What gives! He's a nice lad, a genuine lad. Somebody who we are rather proud of over here, and who deserves to be better known than he is in his homeland. By, the way, what magazine did you say you were from again?'

That was the end of the phone call.

And also the end of her national inquiries.

2

CLIMBING UP THE STAIRCASE

One of the rites of passage for any secondary school pupil growing up in West Lothian during the 1970s was presenting a variety of guidance teachers with an acceptable, namely realistic, career ambition for the rest of your life at the tender age of 14. At Whitburn Academy, where the majority of the students were invariably classified as either dullards or swots and expected to become plumbers and joiners in the first instance, or go to university in the second category, I was in the same class as Louis Di Resta, a feisty, redoubtable character with the sort of attitude which marked him as a natural candidate to star on *The Apprentice* television show if he had been born 25 years later.

One afternoon, the fateful time arrived when we had to discuss our futures with the guidance guru, Alex Sangster (known to his friends as 'Sanny'). The majority of us were flummoxed by his attempts to pin us down on specifics. One boy wanted to drive trains, another thought it would be 'cool' to be a miner, and a couple of the girls had the notion that becoming air hostesses would represent a dream come true. Yet, for the most part, we were floundering around in the dark and I recall the incredulous, scornful look on

Sangster's face when I mentioned an interest in archaeology. Alone of the teenage crew, Di Resta was certain of his destiny in life. 'I am going to be an entrepreneur,' he informed the throng and when the teacher asked how he might achieve that goal, the bold Louis replied masterfully: 'Because my dad owns shops and I will do the same.'

With hindsight, that incident confirmed the ambitious nature and self-belief which has characterised why the Di Restas and Franchittis have enjoyed so much success, on and off the racing circuit. By that stage, Louis was already excelling on the Scottish karting circuit, following in the footsteps of George Franchitti, by travelling to Larkhall, Ingliston, and a range of other arenas, and amassing various championships. Within the next five years between 1975 and 1980, the young Dario would start to appear at these same locations, growing up in a milieu of va-va-voom, surrounded by motors and machinery, and relishing watching his father and his uncle parading their skills and pushing themselves to the limit. 'I must only have been about two or three when my dad started taking me along to the West of Scotland Club – I was in a pram the first time I went – but it was so exciting to watch all the competitors getting ready for action and I remember thinking to myself: 'This is fantastic, this is what I want to do,' Franchitti told me when we discussed his early introduction to the world of speed. 'There was nothing about the experience which didn't seem thrilling to a kid. I used to hear my dad talking about Formula One and enthusing about the likes of Jackie Stewart and Jim Clark and it was in the blood – he loved it, his father had loved it every bit as much, they were speed enthusiasts and, even from an early age, there was something about names like Ferrari and Lotus which just seemed incredibly glamorous. I was hooked from the outset.'

His induction to the sport inevitably led to him owning

a kart and it was Dario's most valued possession, from the moment he reached the grand old age of 10 and launched himself into the ultra-competitive world of junior motor racing. Every weekend, regardless of the weather and no matter how far he had to travel to participate alongside the rest of Scotland's rising stars, he was glowing with anticipation. Several of the officials who worked behind the scenes in karting recall Franchitti as a pint-sized Buzz Lightyear who turned these Sunday excursions into his own private stairway to heaven. 'We knew he had it in him almost from the first moment we clapped eyes on him, because he had this look in his eyes before he drove, this mixture of aggression and determination and control, which is unusual amongst people at the age of 10 or 11,' recalls Stevie Murray, the chief flag marshal at the Larkhall circuit. 'Initially, his dad would drive karts while Dario sat in his pram, with this big, broad grin on his face, as though he had just been showered with presents. But, of course, it wasn't long before he was racing himself and the care and attention to detail which he put into his work was a sign that he was bit exceptional. We also had David Coulthard here and Allan McNish and there was something about all these boys which marked them out as special. They got their hands dirty with the mechanics, they weren't deflated if they lost, but simply rolled up their sleeves and vowed they would come back and win the next time, and that was normally what happened. What was most evident was that, from an early age, they had made up their minds that, come hell or high water, this would be their lives.'

This was a familiar theme from those who witnessed the rise to prominence of the young Franchitti. At three, he had been supplied with his own mini kart, but he possessed something far more valuable in the inspiration and encouragement of his father, allied to the assistance of the unpaid volunteers who keep the conveyor belt rolling at the grassroots of the racing game. Somebody such as Bill Macdonald, the chairman of the West of Scotland Kart Club, for instance, never seeks out publicity or worries himself with pursuing the limelight, but this man has coaxed, cajoled and championed a steady stream of talent through the portals of his organisation and, whether in sunshine, sleet or rain – and these conditions can happen in Larkhall within the space of a few hours – he was the kind of sedulous individual who recognised that Franchitti had abundant potential from his first sighting of the lad. 'He had good equipment, it was always well maintained and well set-up, which comes from the family background, because racing was in the genes and they were all 100 per cent devoted to being as good as they could be.' Macdonald was unsurprised when Dario started hoovering up titles, winning the Scottish Junior Championship in 1984 (at the age of 11), and following that up with the British Junior Championship in 1985 and 1986, prior to serving real notice of his potential by securing the Scottish Senior title in 1988. 'The Franchittis had been involved in motor-sport for years and that knowledge got funnelled down to Dario and his kid brother [Marino] early on and both soaked up information and listened to what they were being told. It was clear from the very, very early days that Dario was crazy about the sport, but one of the things which I remember most forcibly is that he never got carried away or got ahead of himself. Even nowadays, he just turns up here [at the Larkhall circuit] on a fairly regular basis and walks about and doesn't ask to be treated any differently from anybody else. He is a gentleman, a very nice guy – whenever he is here, he will stop and talk to people in the pits and is as far from being aloof as it is possible to be.'

In and around the motoring clubs, Franchitti was in his element. He was less comfortable in his education at Stewart's

Melville College in Edinburgh, if for no other reason than
that it was the kind of establishment where everything ran
on traditional lines and schoolboys with an obsession for
racing cars were out of kilter with with the regimen of rugby
union and cricket which formed the staple diet of the insti-
tution's physical pursuits. Having spoken frequently to
Franchitti, one always derives the feeling that his time there
was to be tolerated rather than recalled with affection. But
there again, perhaps that isn't surprising when one considers
the contrast between the thoroughly modern environment
of competing in karts and the ethos of Stewart's Melville,
whose modus operandi owes more to Harry Potter and
Hogwarts than being down and dirty amidst the Larkhall
set. As if to illustrate the culture clash, when Dario was at
the school, the boys between second and fifth year were split
up into eight houses, which were named after the firths of
Scotland – namely, Beauly, Cromarty, Dornoch, Forth, Lorne,
Pentland, Solway and Tay. Since 2000, the number of houses
has been trimmed to six and these are now named Appin,
Ettrick, Galloway, Kintyre, Lochaber and Torridon. These
various groups compete annually in the 'House Challenge',
an event twinned with girls from the Mary Erskine School,
and the rival participants vie for supremacy in a large variety
of disciplines, ranging from the House Music Competition
to the Inter-House Hockey, with the proceedings culminating
in a climax on Sports Day, with a 4x100m relay between
every house and a Quidditch festival as the denouement.
Actually, I made up that last part, but those who have never
been to fee-paying schools may appreciate that while some
pupils benefit from these activities, others find them bewildering. To be fair, Stewart's Melville does boast an impressive
list of former alumni, including Michael Boyd, the artistic
director of the Royal Shakespeare Company, Tom Fleming,
the actor and television commentator on state occasions,

and a wide range of sports stars, amongst them the British and Irish Lions rugby captain, Finlay Calder, his compatriot, Doddie Weir, the Olympic swimming gold medallist, David Wilkie, and Winter Olympic skier, Finlay Mickel. But though Franchitti features on the list, his exploits had little or nothing to do with his stint at the place which affectionate old boys call 'Stew-Mel' or 'Colleges' – terms which may explain why so many less-privileged generations of rugby teams, many from the Borders, have enjoyed inflicting dollops of pain, both legally and behind the referee's back, when they have travelled to the Stewart's Melville ground at Inverleith for matches.

As it is, Franchitti has been non-committal whenever I have tried to question him about his educational back-ground. Yet at least two of his contemporaries told me, on condition of anonymity, that Dario and Stewart's Melville had gone together as comfortably as Jade Goody and Shilpa Shetty. 'There was a culture of conformity at Stew-Mel which made anybody who didn't like rugby feel pretty uncomfortable,' said one of my respondents. 'It wasn't out-and-out bullying or anything like that, but there was defi-nitely a sense that if you did anything unusual or didn't do what the teachers wanted you to do, you were letting the side down. Bullying doesn't have to involve beating up the class nerd or flushing their heads down the toilet, but it can take more insidious forms, such as indulging in verbal abuse and chipping away at a pupil's confidence by making fun of their name, their background . . . anything which separates them from the crowd. My abiding memory of Dario is that he never looked happier than when he walking out of the school gates at the end of every week.' My second contact was even more direct. 'You have to bear in mind that Dario was a quiet kid from West Lothian, he was a Celtic supporter with not the slightest interest in rugby or cricket and his family were shopkeepers. None of these things are anything to be ashamed of, but youngsters can be incredibly cruel and if they finger you as an outsider, they will never let go. I don't recall Dario ever being in trouble with the teachers, because he kept himself to himself, and he was polite and charming at 12 and 13, which means I am not surprised at how he has conducted himself in the wider world. But he had to put up with insults, being cold-shouldered and little bits of unkindness which were just bullying by another name.'

At least there was an escape back to the world which Dario *did* enjoy and, as his fame increased beyond simply his homeland, he was endowed with a nickname which has persisted to this day. Some labelled him 'Super Dario', and the local newspaper, the *Lothian Courier* used to applaud his feats with the alliterative 'Fantastic Franchitti', but for those of us with a penchant for rock music, he became and has forever remained Dario Speedwagon, which is why this book was so titled. For those with short memories, it had better be explained that, in the autumn of 1980, an American band called REO Speedwagon released the album *Hi Fidelity*, which spawned a clutch of massive-selling hit singles, including 'Keep On Loving You', 'Take It On The Run', 'In Your Letter' and 'Don't Let Him Go,' and although their music was too AOR for some tastes, it perfectly suited the cheesier elements which epitomised the 1980s power-ballad generation – particularly when the band subsequently issued a single called 'Wheels are Turnin' which might have been penned exclusively for Franchitti's benefit.

Better still, as that decade of untrammelled consumerism and the 'Greed is Good' mantra came to a conclusion, Franchitti started to gain tangible benefits from becoming associated with some of the most dynamic entrepreneurial talents in the British motor-sport firmament. Having demonstrated his burgeoning ability in karts, to the stage where he had nothing left to prove, Dario smoothly progressed into the Formula Vauxhall Junior Championship and formed a bond with David Leslie, which was one of the reasons why the young Scot made a rapid impression in his new challenge, winning the championship with four victories in 1991, and earning rave reviews in the process.

Indeed, as Leslie told me in an interview for *Scotland on Sunday*, this was an exciting period to be involved in the motoring business. 'Dario's approach to moving up the ladder has been exemplary – he sometimes nearly drove some of the engineers crazy, because he never stopped asking questions, but suddenly we have a situation where there are a whole new crop of seriously talented young Scottish drivers coming through the ranks and it is fantastic to work with these kids.' Leslie was similarly rhapsodic about Coulthard and McNish, in addition to saluting the efforts of Jackie Stewart, who had established what he described as a 'Staircase of Talent', designed to transform young wannabes into fully-fledged adult competitors. 'We have to do our best to promote this trio, because I have no doubt that they have all the qualities which are required to advance as far as they want to go. I remember Dario was being messed around by an older kid in one Formula Vauxhall race, who was basically trying to drive him off the track. But he didn't let it worry him and he waited on this other youngster to make a mistake and kept on his tail, nervelessly, sure-footedly, until the pressure just got to the other guy and he crashed out of contention. Dario was not interested in shouting and screaming at this boy – he couldn't have cared less. Instead, he went into another zone, sent out the message that nobody was going to muck him about and, half-an-hour later, the victory was in his pocket. It was impressive. No, it was *very* impressive.

With that kind of testimonial, it was hardly a surprise when Franchitti hooked up with Paul Stewart Racing in the 1992 season, where he competed in the Formula Vauxhall Lotus Championship. It was a seminal moment for Dario, given how it allowed him to form a symbiosis with Paul and his father, Jackie, which exists to this day. (On his own website, Franchitti lists his three biggest influences as his parents, George and Marina, and Jackie Stewart). At this time, he also grew better acquainted with his confères, Coulthard and McNish and the triumvirate all benefited immensely from the tutelage of Stewart, the three-times world F1 champion, not simply in gaining financial clout, but from absorbing the myriad lessons which were passed down to them by this canny businessman.

'There had been a long history of Scottish drivers making their name internationally, going right back to the 1940s and 1950s when you had people such as David Murray, Ian Stewart, Bill Dobson, Sir James Scott Douglas, Innes Ireland and Duncan Hamilton blazing a trail, most of them in association with Ecurie Ecosse, and by the time we got to the 1960s, Jim Clark obviously became one of the greatest drivers the world has ever seen,' Stewart told me this year, reeling off names, anecdotes and statistics which proved that even as he approaches 70, his mind is as alert as ever, making it even more disgraceful that Max Mosley, president of the sport's governing body, the FIA, should have been allowed to describe Jackie as a 'certified half-wit' and avoid censure. 'I was the next one to come along after Jim,' Stewart explained, 'and there were one or two others who might have filled the breach after I retired in the early 1970s. But since then, there had been a bit of a gap, and that is why I thought it was important that we created some sort of structure to help promising youngsters realise their ambitions and not, as had happened with a few good kids, be forced to pack in the sport because it was too expensive to keep going.

'That was why we set up the Staircase of Talent and one of the first people to enter it was David Coulthard, who was involved in Formula Vauxhall, the Formula Euroseries, Formula 3000, eventually all the way up to Formula One. Then, during that period, Dario came on board and he quickly showed he was going to be a champion of the future, and Allan McNish also drove for PSR, so it was an excellent breeding ground for these lads and I think they all recognise the stimulus that it provided to their careers, both on and off the track. But what a lot of people perhaps don't understand is how difficult it was to prise sponsorship out of Scotland's leading companies when these guys first arrived on the scene. It wasn't a case of meeting a would-be financier once and then waiting for him to send us a cheque. Instead, I had to keep battering away and using all my powers of persuasion to get the message across that these drivers were worth backing. In the end, I think we were successful and some of the country's biggest companies, from the Bank of Scotland and Walker's to Highland Spring and Kwik-Fit, Marshall's and Irn-Bru, became associated with PSR and the likes of Dario, David and Allan justified that faith, not simply in terms of winning races, but being great ambassadors for their nation.'

This was a staple of the Stewart philosophy: the notion that sporting success cannot be counted purely in terms of cups, medals or appearances on the *Sunday Times* Rich List. In the 1980s, when we first met at Gleneagles, my first thought was that nobody could have met so many famous people or dropped so many names in the space of half an hour, but Jackie is a nonpareil in several respects. Firstly, he has transcended all manner of difficulties, whether in his dyslexia, or the alcoholism of his brother, Jimmy, or the cancer which has afflicted him, his wife, Helen, and Paul, and retained a genuinely sunny disposition. Secondly, although one snooty female journalist said he was about as cool as a blow-torch when he issued his autobiography in 2007, she neglected to mention the fact that Jackie had doled out goody bags, including products by Rolex, Walker's and Glenmorangie, to every member of the press who took the trouble to meet him – in short, he recognises the value of good public relations in a fashion that so many of his motoring peers, whether it be Nigel Mansell, Max Mosley or Ron Dennis, do not. And, thirdly, whatever the background of somebody with talent, Jackie will do his best to help them if he believes they have the capacity to get the nation cheering. And essentially, that was the job which he orchestrated consummately with Dario, David and Allan.

'Clearly, they were all very good drivers and I saw that from the outset, as did several other leading authorities in the sport. But the thing about these three was that they also had dollops of charm, they were personable and fun to be around. You wouldn't always guess that with David, because he has a pretty dry wit, but Dario was one of the sweetest, most even-tempered personalities you could ever wish to meet, and although he could be tough – no, he had to be tough – he was droll and he impressed people whenever he started talking and they understood how much determin-ation and dedication he had. Basically, they were all bright boys. Not perhaps Oxford or Cambridge University mater-ial, but they were street smart and they had worked out that they wouldn't make progress in the motor-sport world unless they mastered life off the track as well as on it.

'That was one of the areas where the Staircase of Talent helped them a lot. We dressed them in suits and ties, we sent them to public-speaking courses, we instructed them in how to arrange their diaries to draw up the right balance between their private lives and what they said and did in the public gaze. They also had to learn to talk to sponsors and potential sponsors, people such as Sir Tom Farmer, Peter Burt and the Marshall family, and Dario was terrific in coming to terms with that part of the job. We told them that they would have to get up before a race and make a speech on what they hoped to do later in the afternoon, and they had to come back later and explain to these tough business people where it had gone right or wrong. That is a hard environment to master, unless you grasp that the PR stuff is part and parcel of the whole motor-sport scene and, to be fair, Dario was brilliant in that regard. Whether it came naturally or not, he had the enthusiasm, and the easy charm to disarm people who weren't even interested in racing cars, and his communication skills were superb. You don't find that too often with 19 and 20-year-olds, but within the next couple of years, he was making the same good impression in Europe and to the Americans and I think that is why he finished up where he did.'

There was one issue which slightly concerned Stewart and that was his protégé's name. Wouldn't it cause confusion with some potential investors to have a chap called Dario Franchitti seeking money from Scottish companies? Fair enough if he was striving to curry favour with Ferrari, but not with Barr's Irn-Bru! To that end, Stewart briefly considered asking Dario – whose name appears on his birth certificate as George Dario Franchitti – to change his monicker to Jock McBain, which would presumably have convinced the world that he was a card-carrying member of the White Heather Club with a passion for haggis and neeps, Angus Og and clootie dumplings and prone to raucous renditions of 'Donald, where's your Troosers?' at the bells on Hogmanay. But it wasn't one of Jackie's wiser ideas. 'It did cross my mind that perhaps Dario didn't sound Scottish enough and that it might be a decent ploy to give him a new identity, which is how we came up with Jock McBain,' says Stewart. 'But, of course, there was no need to do anything of the kind and, as the years passed, it became obvious that Dario Franchitti had a glamour about it which would never have been the case with Jock.'

As far as Franchitti's performance in Formula Vauxhall Lotus was concerned, he was a stern enough judge of his own displays to acknowledge that some things worked better than others, even though he finished his maiden season in a creditable fourth place. In the midst of the campaign, I caught up with him at an Edinburgh garage. We discussed where he saw his short and long-term future, and Dario was typically articulate in addressing the question which seemed to be on everybody's lips. To wit, how quickly would he make the transition to Formula One? 'You can't plan too far ahead in this game, because there are so many different ingredients which have to come together and the whole package has to be right, otherwise you can end up slipping backwards,' said Franchitti. 'To be honest, I am not obsessed at all about F1, because there are many other forms of motoring which I enjoy and I want to taste as many different experiences as possible and the best way to lay down a marker is just to keep winning.

'What can't be argued with is that Jackie Stewart has been an inspiration to me and others like me and he obviously was a superstar of the Grand Prix circuit, and what he doesn't know about F1 could probably be written on a postage stamp. But I am certainly not worrying unduly as to whether I will be in F1 this year, or next, or five years down the line. The fact is I trust the people at PSR to put me on the right course, they have done a fantastic job so far, and they have advised me to spend another season in Formula Vauxhall Lotus, so that is what I am intending to do.

You can't rush things in this sport, you have to be patient and build up your knowledge and work out what you need to improve and I am not 20 until next May, so it's not as if the clock is against me.'

That was in October, 1992. Within a few weeks, Franchitti discovered that he had won the prestigious McLaren/Autosport Young Driver of the Year award, in recognition of the abilities which he exhibited throughout a season of ebbs and flows. In doing so, he was following in the footsteps of Coulthard while, 13 years down the line, his cousin, Paul Di Resta, would collect the same honour, as if testifying to the fashion in which these families have arranged their own staircase of success. Yet if Dario was thrilled to be accorded this accolade, he knew that the popping of flashbulbs and glitzy ceremonials were no substitute for taking steps to mount a serious title bid the following season. In which light, he hired a strength and fitness expert, determined to condition himself to being as mentally and physically sharp as he could be while testing during the winter, and on the next occasion we met, after Christmas in 2003, he was in enviable shape, especially compared to the majority of his compatriots, hunting out the Resolve and Alka-Selzer, following the excess which accompanies the Yuletide festivities.

In these circumstances, it seemed appropriate to talk to some of his peers about how they thought he would fare in 1993. David Leslie had few reservations – Dario, he opined, would be the fellow to beat in the championship. As for McNish, who would subsequently be involved in a dreadful crash at Donington Park, which led to the death of a spectator, he offered the view that Franchitti had shown sufficient ability to launch a sustained charge at the title. In retrospect, this was a golden period for Scottish motor-sport, considering that elsewhere, Colin McRae, was poised to sweep all before him from New Zealand to South America in lifting the World Rally Championship while Coulthard, within 18 months, would be participating in Formula One. It was hardly surprising that Jackie Stewart felt able to joke about the rich seam of resources.

'It's wonderful – isn't it? – how things are coming together. But there again, this is what happens when Scots pull their finger out. Let's face it, wherever there are challenges to overcome or countries to conquer, we are never far from the thick of the action and we have never missed a good war, have we?' he told me, over canapés, mini samosas and other buffet delights in the splendour of Gleneagles Hotel, his eyes twinkling under his tartan bunnet. 'Can I explain the success? Yes, and it has nothing to do with there being something in the water, or any of that nonsense. No, it has all to do with us wanting to prove ourselves and rise above our inferiority complex. You know what Samuel Johnson said about the fairest road a Scotsman ever sees is the road to London. Well, he was talking through his . . . but I am far polite to finish the sentence. Let's just say that when I first travelled to England, I was scared they would think I had heather sticking out of my ears, like one of those country bumpkins you see in the picture postcards. As it is, I think the sky is the limit for David and Dario and Allan – and one or two others [he listed Peter Dumbreck and Andrew Kirkaldy as names to watch] – in the next decade. There was the same wealth of talent in the 1950s, but then things started to slip. But now, hopefully, we have reversed the process and we are in another golden age.'

This was the effervescence and innate ebullience which had endeared the youngsters to Stewart. 'He keeps you on your toes, but when you learn that he wakes up at five every morning and spends the equivalent of a couple of months in the air every year, and never seems short of energy, then you can't help but be inspired,' said Coulthard, during a meeting in Milton Keynes. McNish, meanwhile, provided his analysis. 'Jackie has rammed home the message that we all have to focus on our own strengths and we shouldn't be rigid about our future plans, because it does not matter whether we end up in F1 or rallying, in the DTM or Indycars, as long as we are successful in these branches of the sport,' said the little fellow from Dumfries, on a whistle-stop tour to Glasgow.

That flexibility was one of the factors which appealed to Franchitti and, as the months elapsed, his stock increased in the course of his resounding triumph in the Vauxhall Lotus Championship, where he won half-a-dozen races, left all his rivals trailing in his slipstream, and spoke modestly afterwards about completing another step on the learning curve. 'I have to thank everybody connected with Paul Stewart Racing for this achievement and especially Paul and Jackie for the support which they have shown me in the last few years,' said Franchitti, who was widely tipped in the British press to emerge as a hero of the Grand Prix ranks, alongside Coulthard, before he was very much older.

Yet, as the months went by, and a variety of plans were discussed, it was decided that Dario should shift up to the British Formula Three Championship – the equivalent of the recently-established GP2 – from where it was anticipated that he could put his foot on the throttle in pursuit of a place in Bernie Ecclestone's empire. It didn't seem to have occurred to many people that anything could possibly go wrong. But if 1993 was a halcyon period for Franchitti, nothing was to be as smooth again for years.

3

ALL THE WAY TO AMERICA

Dario Franchitti always seemed like a natural to progress to Formula One. With his Scots-Italian heritage, rugged good looks, letters of recommendation from the likes of David Leslie and Jackie Stewart, and his prodigious driving ability, it seemed a question of not if, but when he would be offered a berth on the Grand Prix circuit. Indeed, having secured the McLaren/Autosport Young Driver award in 1992 and surged to victory in the Formula Vauxhall Lotus series the following year, it might have been supposed that, as he approached 20, he would be staving off approaches from some of the heavy rollers in the F1 world. Yet, for all the talent, the PR savvy, and reports of interest from some in the pit and paddock, his advance to the British Formula Three Championship in 1994 turned into a reality check for Franchitti and any hopes of a Lewis Hamilton-style elevation to Bernie Ecclestone's domain were dashed in disappointing fashion.

It wasn't that Dario was lacking in the basic requirements, but as he told a variety of people, he was searching for a team with whom he could be challenging for honours on a regular basis, not one of the habitual under-achieving organisations within the F1 ranks, whose peak of ambition extended to their cars actually finishing a race. Whether Franchitti knew it or not at his tender age, he could have been accused of limiting his horizons, but there again, there is nothing in the motoring chronicles which insists that Formula One is the be-all and end-all. Dario constantly pushed at the margins and was prepared to test himself in different environments, but never as an also-ran. That was one of the contrasts between him and some of the faceless wonders who appeared content to hover at the back of the F1 grid and collect their pay cheques week in, week out. Financially, it was rewarding, but from a sporting perspective, it betrayed a lack of a true competitive edge, an accusation which can never be aimed at the likes of Franchitti.

However, he would not recall his spell in the Formula Three ranks with any great satisfaction, because, in some respects, the experience simply highlighted how much he still had to learn. The respected race engineer, Nigel Clyde, who works these days with Tiago Monteiro at SEAT in the FIA World Touring Car Championship, formed a close alliance with his compatriot in the early to mid-1990s and has as much knowledge as any observer, both of the potential displayed by Dario, but also the pitfalls he encountered. Clyde had first engineered Franchitti at the Paul Stewart Racing team in 1992, stayed with him for the triumphant '93 season, and subsequently graduated with him to PSR's British Formula Three line-up in 1994 . . . and even finished up back with his confrère at Mercedes' International Touring Car championship in 1996. He quickly spotted Dario's raw energy and range of capabilities, but he also appreciated that some drivers mature quicker than others and that Franchitti would require to be nurtured carefully and not thrust headlong into the spotlight, before he was ready to tackle the challenge.

'He came to us from winning the Vauxhall title.' recalls Clyde. 'Jackie [Stewart] was subsidising him and there were a few other sponsors. '92 wasn't bad – we had some ups and down, but the performance wasn't fantastic. Maybe, he was struggling to adapt to that car, but between then and the following year, he got his head together, hit the ground running, and he was almost a different guy.' He gained a confidence in himself and really attacked the season. He was dominant and, in some places, very quick.

'Dario was one of those drivers who needed coaching, really. Back then there wasn't enough of that and drivers tended to be left to their own devices.' Some might imagine that, under the tutelage of a man of Stewart's calibre, this might be coaching enough, but Clyde doesn't buy into that argument. 'Jackie couldn't be at every test and every race. You needed coaching at every circuit, every test, really hammering it into him. The difference from 1992 was just a bit of confidence, of him driving the car the way it needed to be driven, a bit of maturity even; the car and team were exactly the same.'

After moving to F3, Franchitti's winter testing performances were extremely encouraging, and he and his team-mate, Jan Magnussen, who had moved up from the Vauxhall Lotus Euroseries, were both expected to challenge for the title. Indeed, Dario launched his campaign with a convincing win at Silverstone and seemed to be in the mood to leave all of his rivals straggling. Yet, almost unbelievably, that proved to be a false dawn and his sole success of the entire championship. Magnussen, by contrast, swept to glory with 14 wins from 18 starts and Dario ended up only fourth.

'In winter testing, he looked the better of the two drivers, compared to Jan, and if you had wanted to put money on it, you would have said that Dario would win the title,' declares Clyde. 'Dario maybe is the better driver, but Jan was able to adapt and apply himself better. Dario was better in the winter – and the first race – when temperatures were low, so grip levels were high, because it suited the tyres better. We all thought that this was the way forward, but then he began to struggle. As the season went on, the grip levels dropped, there was more oversteer, less traction, and Dario couldn't deal with it.

'He was always complaining about the car, but he was overdriving it. At every test, you would tell him at the start of the day to just go out and do a few laps to warm up. And he would jump straight to the top of the leader board while taking it easy. Then he would go out and try to push and we would spend the whole day getting slower. It was classic overdriving of cars with high grip and low power and you lose so much momentum that you never pull it back. Jan just drove it, went on a roller-coaster, and never looked back, whilst Dario got more and more frustrated. Jan had this cheeky confidence, and then he was the cat that got the cream, and Dario went into a huge [downward] spiral. He just would not believe that he had as much grip as the others – with hindsight, that is where a good driver coach or a more experienced engineer would have sorted things out.'

At the end of this period, Franchitti received an offer to join the Mercedes touring car team in the DTM, the German-based series, which was one of that country's best-kept secrets in that massive crowds, of 70,000 or 80,000, would regularly flock to the proceedings across the country, yet, outwith the specialist motoring publications, it was accorded about the same attention as junior lacrosse in the Scottish press. Yet, it was a significant step for Franchitti, who, at this stage, was toiling to support himself financially, even with the backing of his family and Stewart, and yet made one of the smartest transitions of his life in hooking up to Mercedes.

'A lot went on between Jackie and Dario [to try and keep things afloat]. The latter didn't have any money – he had one sponsor worth about £15,000. So, as far as Dario was concerned, the Mercedes deal was an easy option,' says Clyde. 'He had no money to go any further in single-seaters and if he stuck with Jackie, it could have collapsed at any moment. It was a money-oriented decision because the Franchittis weren't in a position to do anything themselves.'

While Franchitti and Magnussen [who was also financially restricted in his choices] switched to life in the DTM ranks, they were replaced in PSR's F3 line-up by Dario's future IndyCar rival, Helio Castroneves, and Ralph Firman, who had progressed from the Stewarts' Vauxhall team. Clyde engineered Firman, who had been the fastest driver in Formula Vauxhall, but had thrown away the title, due to mental fragility, and it was the same story in F3. 'I had improved the car a lot, and was into more and more development. Ralph was very quick and could apply himself well, but he just lost the plot in the last three rounds, which was really frustrating, because he had the title in the bag. I wanted a new challenge for 1996. The Stewarts were talking about going into Formula One, and told me to put another year in and maybe we would do something, but I was getting itchy feet by that stage. I put in a call to [the high-performance division of the Mercedes-Benz company] AMG, but I didn't seriously believe that anything would come of it. Then I spoke to [chief designer] Gerhard Ungar, and he said he was interested, but I didn't even think anything of it when I faxed my CV over from PSR just before I went to lunch one day. When I got back, I received a phone call from Gerhard, asking: 'When do you want to start?' As you might imagine, my heart was in my mouth, because I was thinking to myself: 'What have I done?' But I went to see [PSR's] Dave Stubbs and Andy Miller and they told me to do what I wanted to do and then come back to them. So I headed over to Germany at the beginning of January and it was flat-out for three months. Unbelievable! Straight away, Gerhard told me: 'I want you to work with Jan [Magnussen]. I replied: 'No problem', and I think that he was looking for me to protest. He said: 'You know you won't be working with Dario', and I told him that it was okay. I wasn't bothered – I thought it would be nice to work with somebody different. It was going really well with Jan in the tests. And then, just before the first race, at the test leading up to it, Gerhard said: 'I have changed things – you are now on Dario's team'. I said: 'Hang on, you said earlier that I wouldn't be.' But Gerhard tends not to explain himself and just replied: 'That's the way it is.' So I moved across the workshop at short notice from the Warsteiner team to the D2 team and we got ready for the season.'

In his new environment, Franchitti proved more than a match for Magnussen on this occasion, driving a works Mercedes C-Class in the DTM and the related International Touring Car Championship, where he finished fifth and third respectively, whilst exhibiting the prowess which had impressed so many motoring experts on his rise up the ladder. 'Jan was more streetwise and could adapt, but in the right car on the right day, Dario was quicker,' says Clyde. 'We got to grips with the car quickly, hit the ground running, and we were so fast in the ITC we were handicapped, because we were subjected to team orders to help Bernd Schneider in the championship.' As for the question of whether the pair had matured since their previous partnership in 1994, Clyde had no doubts. 'Yes, and I was helping a bit, because I was able to coach him more than before. The data-logging information was better, there was a pool of drivers to look at data from, and Dario and I knew each other very well. There were no problems with saying what we thought – if

I thought the car wasn't being driven as it should be, then I would just tell him, After all, I'd got all the shit about engineering back in 1994!'

However, with the demise of the ITC, Franchitti once more found himself having to ponder his future options. At least he had established valuable connections with Mercedes and had demonstrated that, on his day, he could be a match for almost anybody. Personally, I think this was the stage where he should have been considering a switch to Formula One, because Coulthard had already started to prove his worth, while Nigel Mansell and Damon Hill had bowed out of the Grand Prix ranks, which should have led to Dario gaining an opportunity to parade his abilities. None the less, it didn't happen, although he eventually undertook a test with Jaguar in 2000. Even somebody of Jackie Stewart's acumen seems baffled as to why his protégé kept missing out on a chance to follow in his own footsteps. 'I think he was good material for F1, but perhaps he had stayed too long in America before making the approach to get a test drive,' says the Scot. 'The drive [at Jaguar] went well, but, because of his canniness, he spent the morning getting to know the car, not putting in quick laps. However, there was a mechanical problem which prevented him doing the laps he might have done later, so the laps he did in the morning may not have met the expectations of those in power. He was definitely worthy of more testing, but the reality of life is that you play with the cards which you pick out of the pack. I am sure he would have preferred some of his success to have come in F1, but it wasn't to be and he had done himself proud elsewhere.'

Yet, as far as Franchitti was concerned, what did he have to worry about? When Mercedes placed the 23-year-old with Hogan Racing in the American PPG/CART Champ series in 1997, he had no concerns about travelling to the United

States and rapidly displayed the sangfroid to deal with entering a whole new phase of his life, on and off the track. In some respects, he was glad to have escaped the goldfish bowl that was Britain, where every talented youngster was labelled the next 'Stewart' or the new 'Clark', which was neither fair on the individuals concerned, nor on their predecessors. From the outset, Dario was pragmatic about the Stateside switch and, as he observed, it was not as if there was a vast gulf between F1 and the IndyCar scene, where he would first take his initial footsteps and sufficiently impress his new audience to be winning races and earning millions of dollars within the space of 18 months. In fact, although his debut year might not sound particularly impressive on first glance – he only scored ten points in the campaign, recorded a season-best result of ninth at Surfer's Paradise in Australia, and was 22nd in the title battle – Franchitti possessed both a steeliness and a softly-spoken geniality which struck a chord with many of those following his fortunes. He led in three races – the only rookie to achieve that feat in 1997 – at Gateway in Illinois and in Detroit and Michigan, and was close to gaining points in four other events, despite the reality that he was in nowhere near the best or even the second-best car. But he worked his socks off, bounced back from beginning his campaign by colliding with a wall at Homestead in Miami. He climbed out of the vehicle, shaken but uninjured, and spoke later of how thrilled he was to be involved in such an exciting form of motorsport. Sceptics might respond: 'Well, he would, wouldn't he?', but they perhaps fail to appreciate that Dario, almost from his first day in IndyCars, was convinced that this was more dramatic, more entertaining and certainly more unpredictable than the often sterile Grand Prix world, especially when the best driver and best car are combined, as occurred towards the end of Michael Schumacher's peerless reign.

Some Britons who ventured to the States to witness the spectacle for themselves were left underwhelmed, but then, the majority of these people had no genuine affection for what they were beholding. Those who did turn up at Homestead or Watkin's Glen could recognise that the championship featured an incredible degree of skill, a high risk element and included regular changes of leader and coruscating overtaking moves, neither of which were prevalent in Formula One, or at least not while Herr Schumacher was dominating the pursuit and pounding his rivals into submission with a clinical ruthlessness which commanded respect, but not love.

Wherever one stands on the issue, Franchitti had shown enough flair and ability in his debut season to earn a move to the Team Kool Green organisation for the 1998 campaign and it was with this group and Andretti Green Racing that he attained the pivotal prizes of his profession during the next decade, a period in which he made a mockery of those who had questioned his capabilities by recording regular victories, landing the grand prizes, and becoming one of Britain's highest-paid sports personalities, on the basis of the *Sunday Times* Rich List. From the beginning, whether in testing or in his pre-season media briefings, he was composed and oozed professionalism, to the extent that hardened veterans surveyed his behaviour and smiled knowingly. In January, for instance, when he went to Florida and tested at Homestead and Sebring, Dario ignored the foul weather and produced a lap of 54.9 seconds, which was only six-tenths of a second slower than his older, more experienced team-mate, Paul Tracy, but Franchitti was not in mood to be self-congratulatory. On the contrary, he realised that he would have to up the ante in the weeks ahead. He duly did so with a successful test on the East Course at Firebird International Raceway, completing 166 laps and showing a marked improvement.

'It was good to get back on a road course,' said the man whose first career pole had been secured the previous year on such a circuit in Toronto. 'From a technical standpoint, we are developing the new RK engine and the performance just gets better with every test.' Indeed, the proceedings were virtually without incident, the only note of alarm being sounded during the Sunday session when he slid off the track and finished up in a pool of standing water. Far from being dismayed after this incident, his team officials and engineers were already inclined to speak highly of their new recruit. 'The more I work with Dario, the more I enjoy it,' said their technical director, Don Halliday. 'He is calm and very straightforward and he immediately took the blame for going off the circuit, saying that he missed a shift. But that just goes to show you the kind of guy that he is.'

The praise was all very well, but Team Kool Green required the hard currency of victories to gain credibility and, at least at the start of the season, they struggled to convert pole positions and promising scenarios into tangible rewards. Yet Dario was persistently in the mix, amassing valuable points, serving notice to his rivals that he was growing better with nearly every outing, and all his stakhanovite industry was rewarded when the Scot earned his maiden Champ Car victory at the Road America event at Elkhart Lake in August. He had been forced to wait longer than he would have wished – as had his team colleagues – but there was no doubting the class and conviction which he demonstrated in sweeping to the checkered flag with a comfortable seven-second-plus margin over the runner-up, Alex Zanardi, and the celebrations commenced. At once, Barry Green, the team owner, was in raptures, his emotions ranging from relief to ecstasy. 'It was just a matter of time with Dario. And what a perfect race he drove out there. The pit crew were perfect as well. It is just such a great day for everybody and I am emotionally drained. We have finally got the monkey off our back. To get that second win is going to be very, very hard, but I think that it will be easier than this one.'

Elsewhere, Dario was, as usual, reassuringly delighted without losing the plot. 'The first win is great and I hope that it is the first of many. When I looked at my pit board after the last stop and saw P1 and +10 to Michael (Andretti), I said to myself: "I have seen this before. In Toronto." And I just slowed it down. I was careful with the brakes and just took it easy. The Team Kool Green guys gave me great pit stops all through the race and that enabled me to run away with it. And it feels very good to be where we are.'

If there was a sense of people rubbing their eyes in dis-belief, such was the wait which the organisation had been forced to endure, there was something closer to hysteria a fortnight later when Franchitti, pumped up and prepared to blow away anybody in his path, went out and won the next race on the calendar, the Molson Indy Vancouver, and served up the sort of derring-do which proved the scale of his improvement during 1998. In a reversal of the roles in Wisconsin, Franchitti had to pursue Andretti for a significant period of the afternoon, but on the 80th lap, the ebullient Scot soared past his senior adversary and remained at the helm for the next 28 laps, oblivious to some problems which he later explained had caused him a certain amount of unease. 'The biggest worry of the whole day was some smoke in the cockpit, which started about 20 laps into the race. I could smell smoke, but I thought it wasn't me, it must be somebody else. But then, when I stopped under the yellow, there was smoke everywhere, However, it never got any worse and didn't cause a problem.' Franchitti's heroics in triumphing from pole position – the first driver to do so since Zanardi had managed it 21 races previously (some-thing else which stamped out IndyCars as being different from F1) – brought him $330,000 and another $100,000 for actually winning. 'After the last pit stop, I had to deal with traffic and more yellows, which obviously helped Michael and his fuel strategy. I was thinking: "Come on, give me a break here!" because I didn't think I could get past him. So I just shadowed him, running as fast as I could. From the last yellow to the end of the race, I was running the maximum fuel mixture. I tried to pass once, but it wasn't really on, then I managed to get a better run on him off the last corner into the straight. I got alongside him and that was it. I wasn't sure of the win there at the end when I was behind Michael. I was looking all the time for a way to pass. The brake pedal was going long again and that was worrying me. But then, when I passed Michael, I thought: 'All right!' It's a great feeling to win again, and especially to do so on a street course after being so close in the past. The Team Kool Green guys kind of beat me up when I came into the victory circle. They are big guys and they were hitting me pretty hard – I think they were a bit happy.' The last remark was classic Dario, a combination of understatement and 'Wow', but it was hardly surprising that the team's fans were drinking Canada dry.

These results were a vindication of Dario's decision to take the monumental leap of journeying to a different continent. Back home, of course, there was precious little coverage beyond a few paragraphs, most of it appended with the words 'Bathgate-born'. The time difference didn't help, of course, while the complexities of the IndyCar regime, where fuel strategy and tactics were often as important as driving ability, caused some sports enthusiasts to wonder exactly what was going on in the heat of battle. But those of us who worked for Sunday papers and frequently hung around until news filtered through of how Dario had fared were thrilled with these back-to-back victories and wondered whether he might even snatch the championship as he cranked up momentum in the second half of the summer. Unfortunately, that merely provoked another round of the by-now immensely tiresome inquiry from cynics: 'Okay, when's he coming to F1?'

Yet, on the Le Mans beat in the same season, Dario's compatriot, Allan McNish, was roaring to a memorable triumph in the world's greatest 24-hour race and providing a reminder that the Paul Stewart Racing prodigies were making a serious imprint in motoring all over the world, in contests beyond Grand Prix. McNish, as blithe and bonnie a battler as he was a shrewd judge of human nature, did eventually partake of a brief spell in Formula One, but nowadays, he is feted – and quite correctly – as a master of endurance, a fellow who was happy to drive to the rhythm of the rain on long nights' journeys into days, with only some Jaffa Cakes or Tunnock's teacakes for company. Undeterred by any circumstances, unbowed by accidents or mechanical problems, these fellows, McNish and Franchitti, were passionate in what they did, but somehow, despite possessing wealth beyond the comprehension of the majority of their compatriots, they never relinquished the common touch or the slightly wide-eyed expression of excitement in their hours of triumph, which sprang neither from complacency or arrogance, but simply reflected their joy at being so handsomely rewarded to do something which both of them would gladly have given their eye teeth for when they were growing up.

All of which explained the quiet satisfaction felt by Dario as he emerged with ever more mature performances throughout the 1998 IndyCar campaign. Success at Elkhart Lake and in Vancouver was soon enough followed by his third win of the year in the inaugural Texaco Grand Prix of Houston and while the event may have been rendered slightly farcical by the overhead conditions, which were like something from the film *The Day After Tomorrow*, as thunder, lightning and torrential rain reduced the race to 70 laps, you can only win the event in which your competing and let the dice fall as they may. Yes, it was the case that 100 laps were originally scheduled, but improvising and thinking on your feet were and remain essential ingredients of this sport. Franchitti and his support staff responded better to the elements than anybody else, with him crossing the line ahead of Alex Zanardi by a narrow margin of 0.646 seconds, whilst Tony Kanaan ended up in third, as the paths of some of Dario's best buddies began to intertwine. One leading US motoring journalist considered this to be one of Franchitti's best displays, because he knew what he had to do, starting from second on the grid, and duly showed a decisiveness and ruthless quality which wasn't always apparent in his psyche by surging past Greg Moore on the first corner, even as the weather forced the race into a single-file opening on rain tyres. 'It was mighty impressive, because he didn't hang around for a moment, he just pounced like a sprinter out of the blocks, and although Moore must have guessed what was coming, he never stood a chance,' said Jeremy Shaw, a fellow who isn't given to the type of Murray Walker-style commentary which once had Clive James remarking it was like listening to a man whose trousers had just caught fire. 'As soon as Dario arrived in the United States, he attracted favourable attention, because you soon discover who are the big mouths and who are the people who let their actions do the talking and Dario was firmly in the latter camp. Before he stepped into the Team Kool Green set-up, they were in danger of being dismissed as an outfit who couldn't buy a victory, but he changed all that in a couple of months. And he did so without making a big deal about it, which some of us thought was pretty neat.'

Instead, Franchitti rolled with the punches and kept his concentration in an incident-packed event. Accidents proliferated, and were responsible for five of the six cautions in the race, and when Paul Tracy's vehicle made contact with his team-mate, Franchitti, there was a danger that the KOOL crowd might succumb to friendly fire. Yet, unperturbed by the episode, which resulted in Tracy spinning into a wall and suffering irreparable damage to his suspension, Dario motored on, and would not be denied another checkered flag, even though the skies had opened, and a near-deluge accompanied his sprint to his goal.

As a consequence, Franchitti moved up to third in the championship standings, on 142 points, just six behind Jimmy Vasser, and he was understandably bullish, even if he confessed that the elements had made the Texas contest akin to a lottery. 'It was a very difficult day, because of the conditions all the time. It was like an ice rink out there at the start, then it dried out and became very grippy again, then back to the ice rink once more,' said Dario. 'My team called an excellent race for me, telling me when to pit for slicks and come back in for rain tyres, so full marks to the guys for keeping on top of the situation. We've scored a hat-trick now with three wins and I hope that they keep coming, because it is a great feeling.' Those words, which typically underplayed Franchitti's starring role in transcending the horrible conditions, were followed up by a warm tribute from Barry Green, who declared: 'Dario drove an excellent race under some of the most difficult conditions which I have ever seen. It is a credit to all of the team for preparing a great car, calling a great race and giving Dario excellent pit stops. The team had been performing well all year and it was very frustrating when we couldn't get a win under our belts. But now we have three and with two more races to go, we have the confidence to keep on winning and, as you can imagine, we can hardly wait until the next event.'

It was engrossing action, which had captivated an increasing number of Americans, even if the championship leaders were now, respectively, a Swede, Kenny Brack, and a Scot. Then, just as if to accentuate the global nature of the title, the action switched to Australia in the middle of October, which can be one of the most gorgeous times of the year in that beautiful country. It's warm but not so warm as to be oppressive. Springlike, but not so changeable as we have grown accustomed to in Britain. No wonder that whenever Franchitti ventured Down Under, it was with a keen sense of anticipation and expectation, and, considering the large number of expatriate Scots and Italian immigrants who had settled in Oz, he was always assured a hearty greeting.

In this instance, the pressure had intensified, because Dario had advanced far ahead of Tracy in the IndyCar series, which is hardly what would have been envisaged at the start of the campaign. Yet, if he was feeling any nerves, he kept them to himself and knuckled down, in the midst of Surfer's Paradise, to consolidating his summer advances. As it materialised, he fell just short of another victory, finishing second to Zanardi, whose fluctuation between wonderful and woeful carried on unabated. Yet, to put the outcome in context, this was Dario's sixth podium of the season, and once again he rose above a litany of cautions – seven in total – which transformed the contest into a timed two-hour race and pushed Zanardi all the way, before the latter scraped home by 0.322 seconds. Once more, Franchitti had claimed pole position in qualifying – his fifth of the year – and he led for the opening 13 laps until Michel Jourdain's spin brought out the first full-course yellow and, in the ensuing round of pit stops, Zanardi was quicker to return to the circuit and established a narrow advantage which he never subsequently ceded. Yet, elsewhere, it was far from a humdrum affair, with the hapless Tracy experiencing another dismal afternoon. The Canadian driver was struck from behind by Michael Andretti in a collision which punctured his left rear tyre, severely damaged his suspension and grievously bruised his ego, if his thunderous expression at the death was any indicator. His problems were in marked contrast to Dario's consistency, although any motoring aficionado will be aware that these things usually go in cycles. The trick is to profit on the good times and, by the close of the proceedings in Australia, Franchitti had secured another 16 points and climbed up to second in the championship, ahead of the finale in Fontana. He had also surged 12 points clear of Jimmy Vasser, who failed to finish, and although there was no prospect of claiming the title, Franchitti was entitled to believe that he had laid down a significant marker for the future. 'We were just a fraction slower than Zanardi on the first stop and that was the difference out there today. The only chance I had was on one of the re-starts. Other than that, I couldn't get close enough. Car to car, I think my KOOL car was quicker than Alex today. But he had nothing to lose and I had a lot to lose,' said Franchitti later. 'So, basically, second place today is good. We have moved up to second in the championship and have a bit of a gap over Jimmy. You can't win them all, but it would be great if you could.' If he was exuberant, Tracy, who was nearly 100 points worse off than his younger colleague in the standings, was morose. 'Michael [Andretti] hit me in the rear on the back straightway and it was so bad that I was left driving with only front brakes. Doing 190mph down to 30mph for the corners with no rear brakes – well, it's just not safe out there. I'm disappointed for the Kool team, because I had a good car, and we were just trying to make the necessary fuel mileage to finish on the podium, but it wasn't to be and that has been the story for me in the last few races.'

They were a disparate duo, but Franchitti couldn't afford to be overly sympathetic. He had his own challenges and motivations to pursue and, regardless of how sociable and genial Dario was when out of the cockpit, he was no shrinking violet when strong words were required or he was facing down intimidating tactics from a rival. On several occasions when we met, he was charm personified, but he bridled at those who maintained that his vocation wasn't a proper sport. Those who harboured such a prejudice, he argued, should try their hand sometime at controlling a racing car at 200mph in the midst of a rain storm. True, he might have been a surprisingly diminutive figure to those who encountered him – so for that matter, is Michael Schumacher, whom I met at Silverstone in 1998, prior to a rain-soaked British Grand Prix on the same Sabbath day that France trounced Brazil in football's World Cup final – but Franchitti was muscular, as fit as any footballer, and generally exuded the impression that he would be tough man to beat if he ever showed up on a modern equivalent of the programme *Superstars*, where Kevin Keegan famously fell off his bike in the 1970s. In fact, as I write, this show has recently been revived, with Jim Rosenthal hosting a range of powder-puff contests between a collection of has-beens and minority sports competitors. It should have been left in its original condition, but these days, anything and everything which can be revived *is* revived, hot on the heels of the success of *Doctor Who*. Franchitti had other, better things to do than surround himself with distractions. Even after three wins, he urgently wanted to chase a fourth.

So, he prepared meticulously for the IndyCar denouement, which was the 500-mile epic at the California Speedway. In advance, he spoke admiringly of the sterling work which had been implemented behind the scenes by the likes of Barry Green, allied to a tremendous amount of labour from a small army of engineers, technicians, telemetry experts, men who would never be famous, but whose expertise and dedication ensured that when Franchitti climbed into the car, he was both safe and ultra competitive.

Sadly, however, there are only so many scenarios which can be predicted in advance and if something goes kaput, there is nothing any racing driver can do to retrieve the situation. Dario had been as reliable as clockwork in the second half of the Indy campaign, but he suffered glitches at exactly the wrong time as his season ground to a halt in slightly anti-climactic circumstances. Starting from eighth on the grid – the Saturday had not gone 100 per cent to plan either – he had orchestrated a thrilling resurgence and progressed to second place, only for his engine to blow 112 laps into the event. At a stroke, his aspirations were dented. He could do no better than 22nd and, just to cap a mediocre finale for the KOOL organisation, Tracy seemed to be poised for a morale-boosting victory, before making the sort of error which leaves those on the periphery raging at how pressure can occasionally transform the most talented characters into novices. Ideally positioned to collect a win, he was only four laps away from his objective while steeling himself for the restart after the eighth caution of the afternoon. It was a state of affairs which called for calmness and composure with Tracy sitting in front of Greg Moore, Jimmy Vasser and Alex Zanardi, whose hopes rested on whether they could jump ahead of the leader from the ensuing green flag. Yet, as the pace car lights went out, Tracy pressed down too hard on the throttle and spun off the course, leaving the way open for Vasser to win the race and rub in the pain by overtaking Franchitti in the rankings, which was a dispiriting conclusion to what had been a momentous tussle.

When the dust had settled, there was still ample consolation for Franchitti, although it must have stuck in his throat that Vasser's belated exploits saw him pick up not only $1m for the victory, but also $500,000 for coming second in the IndyCar table. But, in the final analysis, it had been a meritorious display of consistency and sustained excellence from the Scot, who had enhanced his reputation, brought a stack of honours to his employers, and proved that he had been right to accept the challenge of settling down in America when the offer came along. 'You never know how this thing could have turned out, but the KOOL car was running really, really well out there. There wasn't any warning on the engine. I just heard a noise and then the engine let go. But I think the team did a terrific job this weekend, having run so badly at Michigan earlier this year,' said Franchitti, who had become a master of phlegmatic reflection. 'We have all worked really hard since then and we were running up front today. I have also learned a lot about racing on Superspeedways since Michigan and it really felt great to be competitive all weekend and to be challenging for the win. I am just disappointed we could not finish the race.'

In the wider context, he was relatively unconcerned about losing a place – and a six-figure sum in dollars – in the championship. 'I would have loved to finish second, but I don't care about the money. One or two hundred thousand up or down doesn't really matter. Third overall is still a good reflection of the kind of season we had and the bottom line is that we were *the* team to beat in the second half of the season.'

His serenity was a world removed from the angst of Tracy, who could offer no mitigating circumstances for his gaffe at the climax and was also conscious of the fact he had only wound up 13th in the championship; an apt position, given the fashion in which a variety of issues had nagged away at his resolve since March. 'From my standpoint, I dropped the ball. The guys in the team worked their butts off this season and they deserved to finish on a high note, but I messed up. I just tried to do the restart the way I had done the previous one and get a good jump, but it just backfired on me,' said the 29-year-old. 'It was my mistake and I am just sorry for the guys and everybody from KOOL, Klein Tools, Firestone and everybody else involved with Team Kool Green.'

It was far from the outcome which Barry Green would have expected, but privately, some of the doubts surrounding his enterprise had been expunged. Most encouraging of all, he knew that this fellow Franchitti was the real deal and would be capable of vying for titles in the future. None of which entirely glossed over the last-day glitches. 'We can't lose sight of the fact that we had two fast cars, two fast drivers, we ran up front and we had a good chance of winning it today' he said. 'We obviously made a mistake four laps from the end, but this is not a low day for us. Paul had to be very aggressive on the restart to hold them off, he was attempting to do that, and it just got away from him. I guess that just about sums up our season. But Paul has made a big difference to the team and we will be back next season with a big punch.' Green's thoughts were already turning to 1999.

'It was a tremendous drive from Dario today. It was only his third 500-miler, and he was fast: he was cruising: he was in control. Unfortunately, we had an equipment failure, but Dario knows now that he can race up front on these Superspeedways and that was a question going into this race which he has definitely answered. In fact, he has been doing that all year and to get three wins is terrific for him and for Team KOOL Green.'

It was a rational assessment of a campaign which had

begun inauspiciously, but which had substantially improved as the months had elapsed. The season's ebbs and flows also emphasised the element of surprise which marked the IndyCar circuit and although there would be new challenges in the following year for Franchitti – not least the arrival of a rumbustious rookie called Juan Pablo Montoya – he was replete with confidence and enthusiasm when we spoke towards the end of the year. Perhaps this was hardly surprising. Here, after all, was a young man who had banked millions of dollars, a Celtic-daft football fan associated with a Kool Green team, in the season when his heroes prevented Rangers from creating a piece of history by winning ten league titles in a row, and he had not so much announced his arrival on the Indy circuit as knocked down the door with a battering ram. Ultimately, he would have to face up to the rumours linking him with Formula One, particularly given Jackie Stewart's involvement in setting up a new Grand Prix organisation, but Dario was at ease with himself and repeated his mantra that it would be futile to settle for a mid or lower-table berth in F1 for the sake of it, when there were so many incentives to launch a fresh ascent towards the Indy summit.

Consequently, one of the less surprising announcements happened on December 19, 1998, when Barry Green confirmed that Dario and Paul would be returning to compete for his team in the CART FedEx Championship series in 1999. The Canadian had signed a three-year agreement, while Franchitti had pledged himself to two more seasons, but there was nothing sinister in that arrangement. Instead, Dario was the sort of person who liked to keep his options fluid and he preferred the shorter-term contracts to being tied to anything indefinitely. 'Having Paul and Dario return as our drivers will make us even stronger next season,' said Green, whose candour and refusal to indulge in favouritism for one driver over another was in marked contrast to how business was being conducted in F1, where David Coulthard had controversially slowed down on the last lap of the 1998 Australian Grand Prix and allowed Mika Hakkinen to claim victory. 'Success has come quickly for KOOL when you consider that this is only the company's third year of sponsoring open-wheel racing and only the second in the FedEx Championship series for the PPG Cup. The successes achieved are remarkable when compared with those of other sponsors, who have accomplished much less, despite significantly longer involvement in major sponsorships. But we can't stand still. If we want to be successful over time, we have to devote a good deal of effort to developing drivers and achieving excellent results from top to bottom of the team.'

There was no denying the impact which the dynamic between Franchitti and Tracy, allied to the industry of Green, had steered the company into uncharted waters. There had been some surprise, initially, when Franchitti touched down in the States and, for years afterwards, some people would either think he was an Italian or would have no idea at all about his origins. But if this was symptomatic of the often parochial nature of American society, it hardly mattered a jot to the man from West Lothian, who had blended seamlessly into the background, except in the one area where he needed to be forward. Less than five years on from his problems in the British F3 Championship, his life had advanced to higher ground and he was maturing, both as a person and as a driving force in his milieu. The next year would provide sterner examinations in both regards, but Franchitti gave the impression that he was up for the fight.

4

JUAN, GREG AND ASHLEY

If his early experiences on the CART circuit convinced Dario Franchitti that he could expect no favours in his bid to wrest as many victories as possible from his rivals and launch a credible title challenge, the 1999 championship campaign was the season when he stamped his imprint and authority on his Stateside contemporaries. It was also the year when he met Ashley Judd, and the pair's life was changed in a twinkling. And it was the time when he lost one of his best friends, Greg Moore, as if some divine meddler upstairs was trying to balance Dario's reserves of joy and despair.

By this stage, he had adapted well to the contrasting demands of his CART schedule, but he appreciated that he faced a gruelling itinerary, with plenty of events scheduled on different circuits and in diverse countries, as the sport sought to enhance its appeal. In some respects, this was unsuccessful – and one leading British driver once remarked to me that he found the whole Indycar scene about as attractive as root canal treatment – but few people with open minds could have failed to be intrigued and occasionally horrified by the dramatic and harrowing manner in which the protracted season unfolded.

It wasn't simply the contrasting experiences which confronted the likes of Dario, Tony Kanaan, Gil de Ferran, Patrick Carpentier and Michael Andretti as the weeks passed by, but also the remarkable debut of a young Colombian rookie, Juan Pablo Montoya, which evoked widespread coverage and drew support from beyond the cognoscenti. An unprepossessing figure who would subsequently switch to Formula One, Montoya could veer between the inspired and the inept, occasionally within the space of a few laps, but he was great copy for a sport which had previously too often sang to the tune of 'Send in the Clones', and the more that he and Franchitti were pitted in an engrossing battle of wills, which extended to a ghastly climax, the greater the level of public acclaim.

Even by that stage, Dario had forged close allegiances with most of his on-track rivals, and life for these twenty-something bachelors was as hectic out of their vehicles as within the cockpit. Indeed, he and Moore, Kanaan and Max Papis were sufficiently enamoured of each other's company that they soon became known within their sport's ranks as the 'Brat Pack', a nickname which had originated from the famous confederation of Frank Sinatra, Dean Martin, Sammy Davis Jnr and Peter Lawford, whose hedonistic activities brought a dash of notoriety to the Hollywood scene in the 1950s and 1960s.

Certainly, there was nothing half-hearted about the racing quartet's relish for joining le beau monde on the party circuit. And whether becoming involved in judging beauty pageants in Australia, discussing the finer points of a new kid on the golf block called Tiger Woods or taking Harley-Davidsons for a ride up the California coast, Dario was luxuriating in the American dream, working and playing hard in equal measure, proving to his peers that he could both shoot the breeze and fire himself up for the Champ Car challenge without relinquishing his grip on either a social or sporting existence.

'We all kind of get along,' said Franchitti, of his fellow aspirants, with Moore, in particular earning his respect and admiration as one of life's natural good guys. 'We are different in a lot of ways, but we are also incredibly similar. When we are on the road, they are like my family and it sort of clicks.' But when the qualifying starts in the countdown to a race, they are the opposition. We can all flick that switch, but that's no reason for us not to be friends again at the finish." As if to illustrate the point, while emphasising the rivalry between them, there were private wagers within the group, and Franchitti and Moore shared a $5 bet on who would take pole position at the Surfer's Paradise Grand Prix in 1998. Dario duly secured first place and wasted no time in collecting the ante. 'The first thing I did after getting out of the car was to go looking for Greg. He's a very confident person and he thought, for sure, that he would take pole. But I enjoy beating him and the rest.' Shortly afterwards, though, Moore invited Franchitti to spend a week at his family's home in Vancouver, British Columbia, and the rapport between the Scot and his Canadian hosts testified to the bond which had been established. 'Because we are on the road so much, it's nice to have friends and people you can trust and interests you can share,' said Moore. 'We are all similar ages, we enjoy hanging out together and this sport has been our passion for years, so there is that connection.'

In the period before these charismatic characters began imprinting themselves on the US consciousness, their pursuit had toiled to gain widespread recognition. But, as the Brat Pack grew ever more newsworthy, the *New York Times* reported on the phenomenon in terms which demonstrated that Dario & Co. had managed to make a breakthrough.

'To a man, they are dedicated at their job and they are very good at what they do, but they just happen to be young, single and free to enjoy some of the world's most stimulating cities, from Miami to Monterey,' wrote Tarik El-Bashir. 'While many of their nocturnal adventures are kept secret by the pack's members, there are plenty of wild nights which have become conversational fodder in the garage area. Take, for instance, the night after Franchitti's first-ever victory at Elkhart Lake, where the drivers celebrated at the best (and only) tavern in town. At 4am, the party was just getting started. Needless to say, Franchitti, was not on his [scheduled] 8am flight home to Scotland. And Papis stopped to take a nap on the lawn in front of his hotel – it was, after all, on the way back to his room. 'The next morning, they found me in bed – wearing all my clothes,' said Papis, the group's self-proclaimed leader. 'You can give yourself freedom, but you have to know your limitations at the end of the day. I'm not a party animal, I am a human being. But trying to achieve goals in life shouldn't prevent you from enjoying life as well.'

It was a mantra which appealed to Dario, encompassing as it did both his sangfroid and joie de vivre and the antics of the quartet throughout their hectic induction to the Indy circuit were worthy of something from a Damon Runyon short story.

Granted, it was a slow-burning film noir, which required patience from viewers, but the central protagonists made their identity known from the outset when the title commenced at Homestead in Florida on March 21. Indeed, this was a microcosm of what lay in store with Moore, the 23-year-old Canadian, capitalising on an excellent opportunity to win, following quick pit work from his crew after an accident on Lap 111, involving Adrian Fernandez, who blew a tyre with 40 laps remaining. During the early stages,

Franchitti led the event, and had amassed an eight-second lead until Scott Pruett collided with the Turn One wall, at which point he surrendered his advantage and even slipped out of the top five, prior to making up lost ground as the finish beckoned. Eventually, Moore was the victor, managing to hold off Andretti, with Dario in third, but the myriad fluctuations which characterised the tussle offered a hint of how a group of disparate drivers would taste all kinds of conflicting emotions as the heat of the championship intensified.

Fernandez, for instance, the man who had suffered misfortune in the opener, emerged triumphant in the next race, almost entirely dominating the proceedings, but still requiring a couple of late yellows to guarantee his success, and took the checkered flag under caution, as the prelude to his gearbox seizing up before he could even drive into the winner's enclosure. 'It could have been close – that is what my guys told me – but I saved fuel all day and that turned out to be critical,' said Fernandez later, with the look of a man who recognised that matters could have been very different if the race had stretched even another few hundred metres. 'I was thinking to myself: 'Should we pit or should we stay out?' But I had to tough it out at the end. I couldn't even look at the fuel gauge.'

Elsewhere, a madcap scramble in and out of the pits by some of the competitors preceded a frantic scrap, with Moore enduring a spectacular spin, de Ferran producing a highly-charged rearguard action to wind up in second spot, ahead of Christian Fittipaldi, Moore, and Andretti, with neither Franchitti nor Montoya enjoying their afternoons at the Twin Ring Motegi in front of a crowd of 60,000, who made noise enough for 600,000. Yet if there were any sceptics among the congregation, who thought that the pre-season publicity for Montoya had been nothing but hype, they discovered that he was the real deal as April progressed into May, with a series of stunning performances from the South American. His stratospheric streak commenced in Long Beach in California, where he became the first rookie to win a CART event in 38 starts since Alex Zanardi had triumphed at Laguna Seca in 1996. It was a stellar showing from Montoya, who grabbed the lead from Kanaan with just over half of the race remaining and stormed on to a convincing 2.805-second win over Franchitti, who himself was in scintillating touch for much of the day, exhibiting how both men were sparking off one another. 'The first stint in the car was the toughest, you have to believe me about that,' said Dario. 'We blistered the back tyres pretty badly. Juan passed us at the restart and then the three of us – TK, myself and Juan – were going at it nose to tail. It was just a case of doing my best to keep Juan within my sights, but I don't think I had the car to do that today. Still, we gained some good points and we will get things together and move on to Nazareth.'

By now, Franchitti had grown accustomed to mingling with the Hollywood set and the list of celebrities at the Long Beach Grand Prix included Nicolas Cage, Anthony Edwards, Tim Allen, Patricia Arquette and country-music singer, LeeAnn Rimes. His contacts book was bulging with every passing week, and he was unfazed by meeting and greeting A-listers, even if his priority clearly lay in what happened on the tracks, not off it. Yet, the more thespians he encountered, the more parties and social functions he found himself being invited to attend. 'You can't take that world too seriously, you have to concentrate on the day job and if you meet nice people on the journey, then that is a bonus,' he told me when we chatted at the beginning of the 1999 CART crusade. 'All through my life, I have had the attitude that you should treat people as you find them and that applies whether you are in Scotland or in the United States. Basically, I quite enjoy putting a name to a face and sometimes it is good to be talking about things other than motor-sport. But I don't kid myself that I belong on a red carpet. That's not what I am about.'

Montoya, on the other hand, was savouring his rapid rise to fame. After Long Beach, he and his Target/Chip Ganassi team progressed to Nazareth in Pennsylvania and repeated the pyrotechnics with another success, which opened up clear water between himself and Franchitti, who could do no better than eighth. Worse still, from Dario's perspective, when the participants advanced to Brazil on May 15, Montoya carved his name into the record books by becoming the first-ever rookie to record a hat-trick of consecutive wins, with a coruscating performance at the Nelson Piquet International Raceway. The catalyst for his third triumph was when he out-braked the front-row starters, Fittipaldi and Franchitti, on the second of 108 laps and, thereafter, led for the remainder of the event, sealing his berth in the archives with a majestic air of superiority, which seemed to be saying, à la Bart Simpson, to his would-be adversaries: 'Eat my Shorts.' Franchitti, to his credit, retained his sangfroid in coming second, but the gap between him and his younger rival had risen to 14 points and if he wasn't exactly frazzled at the outcome, his demeanour and words intimated that he knew he was in one hell of a battle. 'The start was very import-ant today and you have to say that Juan stole a march on us. Once he was in the lead, it was never going to be easy to catch him up. We had a great stop on the first stop, then it was a case of doing our best to conserve fuel and I was able to go two or three laps more than Juan, which I thought was an advantage. Our biggest problems were on the restarts after my shifter broke on the third lap and we had to make the best of the situation. In one sense, it is nice to have more points in the bag, but second is not why we are all here. No, I want to be in that [Montoya's] seat and the responsibility is now with us to stop him building up any more wins and get back the initiative.'

The trouble was that even though Montoya couldn't keep the sequence going at Madison in Illinois, a fortnight later, the pressure had markedly increased on the likes of Franchitti, whose aspirations were shattered when he collided with his team-mate, Paul Tracy on lap 147, and was unable to continue in an event where the veteran Andretti secured the spoils in front of Helio Castroneves. On the sidelines, the actor, Paul Newman, responded to the outcome as if he had just been showered with a barrowload of Oscars, while Mario Andretti, employing the pithy language for which his family were famous, commented: 'It has been a very dry spell, and it really made the guys crazy. But nothing can be as good as this.' Even allowing for the euphoria of the moment, this was ever so slightly over-egging the pudding, but that was part of CART's appeal. Namely, that regardless of how logical and well-rehearsed the majority of the drivers were in discussing logistics, telemetry and pit strategy, most of them were nothing but overgrown schoolboys whenever they took the checkered flag. Franchitti, on the other hand, was far less inclined towards histrionics and slapstick, and basked in his Invisible Man status. Later in his career, it would gradually become irksome to be simply taken for granted. But, for the moment at least, he could slip under the radar and stick to his priorities.

What *was* galling was the fact that he had still to register a victory in 1999 and Dario was entitled to have mixed feelings when his Team Kool Green colleague, Tracy, crossed the finish line with just enough fuel in his tank at the Milwaukee Mile in the next race to claim the 14th victory of his career in the Miller Lite 225. It was a contrasting experience for Tracy and Franchitti: the former enjoyed an emphatic success with a 5.880-second advantage over Moore and Gil de Ferran. But the latter started in fourth and only limped home in ninth, following a series of self-inflicted problems. He had actually led the proceedings from laps 47–69 and was running in second when he entered the pits for his first stop, but ran over an air hose in Tracy's pit box and, consequently, was slapped with a black-flag penalty, which pushed him to the back of the lead lap in 14th position. As if to reaffirm his positive qualities, he sped back up through the field and climbed as high as seventh, but the glitches continued, both in handling and with his brakes. Ultimately, this wasn't a day to linger in the memory, but he did his utmost to sound happy for Tracy. 'It was a great victory for Paul and he deserved it. He has been trying to break down the door for a while and it has finally happened, and I am really delighted for the guy. Personally, my crew had a difficult time of it. But we got some points and took some points away from the championship leader [Montoya]. We had a couple of problems which really affected us. I ran over an air hose, for which I put up my hands, and we lost the rear brakes towards the end, which wasn't my fault. I couldn't slow the car down in the corners and could not stop it in the pits. I don't know why it happened, but it kind of ruined our day. However, we are still in there fighting and we have to hope for better fortunes when we get to Portland in three weeks.'

Franchitti's mood had been enhanced for reasons which had nothing to do with motors. In February, 1999, prior to the launch of the CART Championship, he had attended the wedding of Jason Priestley, the star of the TV programme *Beverly Hills 902102* and had been introduced by Greg Moore to an actress, Ashley Judd, with whom he forged an immediate rapport. She was almost five years his senior, but the woman born Ashley Tyler Ciminella – the daughter of Naomi Judd, a well-known American country-music singer and Michael Ciminella Jnr, a marketing analyst for the horse-racing industry – was vivacious company. She was interested in sports, arts and a variety of political, social and environmental causes and was, and always had been, a million miles removed from the stereotype of the typical vapid Hollywood starlet. Quietly, discreetly, the pair from different worlds began dating and although they had to engage in a long-distance relationship for much of the courtship, Franchitti and Judd became an item. The duo were relaxed and comfortable without needing to make their affair public.

With hindsight, it was hardly a surprise that the pair discovered an instant simpatico. Dario had consistently demonstrated that he wasn't remotely interested in living up to the swaggering, roistering image of so many racing drivers, for whom a one-night stand is being unduly faithful, while Judd, who had previously been linked with singers, Lyle Lovett and Michael Bolton, and actors, Matthew McConaughey and Robert De Niro, had the good sense to appreciate that she could do without devoting the rest of her life to narcissists. Instead, she was proud to be a feminist, a Christian who 'wanted to take Jesus back from the right' and a Democrat, who could sniff out Republican cant at 1000 metres and recognised that when big business talked about 'forest management firms', it was a weaselly-worded euphemism for deforestation. And, later, as she and Dario grew closer, she spelled out the values which had endeared him to her. 'He's sensitive, he is caring and he has a strong code of ethics, and knows what is right and wrong. The other night, he went to see some film which was filled with guns and explosions and violence and the woman sitting next to him in the cinema had two children under the age of five with her. And Dario just turned to her and said: 'I'm sorry, but you have to leave. You can't have these children in this movie.' It was great.' And it was also a sign that Franchitti was no slack-jawed Rainier Wolfcastle fan, but a rounded member of the human race.

Back on the track, the next chapter in the CART saga yielded fresh disappointment for Dario, whose travails at the Grand Prix of Cleveland in finishing a sorry 25th – due to a throttle linkage problem – were compounded by another win for the increasingly confident Montoya, who proved the most efficient at overcoming the adverse weather conditions during a rain-saturated afternoon. The Colombian, whose exploits were already gaining wider attention across the world and attracting the gaze of the F1 panjandrums, was strong and clinical in everything he did, leading for 76 of the 90 laps and surging to a 10.604-second victory over de Ferran, Andretti and Paul Tracy. And, although he sought to dampen expectations in the aftermath, it was clear that he had graduated beyond thoughts of making a good first impression to believing he would lift the title. 'The race went really well when it was very wet, but when it starts to dry, the car doesn't work so well on wet tyres. The same thing happened to me at Portland last week and it is something we have to work on in the future,' said Montoya. 'All the same, we had some troubles and we made some mistakes early in the year, but now things are much better. The Honda engine is working well, and while I know that there is still a long way to go, I am seriously thinking in terms of winning the championship and I am very happy.'

Franchitti, in contrast, cut a slightly forlorn figure, and with good reason, because whereas Montoya had extended his lead, Dario had slipped back to third in the CART rankings, on 85 points behind de Ferran (87) and the leader on 112, which meant, as Dario acknowledged, that there was

little room left for error. But if that made for a depressing
return home, there was just as little to celebrate at Elkhart
Lake in Wisconsin, where the woes of both the Team Kool
Green drivers, Tracy and Franchitti, mounted, with the
former only crawling to a poor 11th and the Scot not finishing
at all, following yet another technical gremlin, which left
him with a mountain to climb. His sole crumb of comfort
lay in the fact that Montoya also suffered, allowing another
South American, Christian Fittipaldi, of Brazil, to earn his
maiden success in the Indycar series, taking the checkered
flag narrowly ahead of his colleague, Andretti. Yet what was
most frustrating for Dario was the smoothness with which
he progressed for almost half of the contest, only to be
afflicted anew with a kick in the teeth. Both he and Tracy
were in the top five when the malaise struck, forcing
Franchitti to pit and examine the problem, but he didn't
bother trying to resume his challenge and despite doing his
utmost to sound upbeat in the subsequent press conference,
he was now down to fourth in the CART battle – behind
Montoya, Andretti and de Ferran – and, for all his civility
and courteous behaviour in adversity, these chats were
starting to resemble Baldrick's cunning plans. 'The car was
perfect today, and we were the fastest car out there until
the mechanical problem arose. I think it was a turbo problem,
because we had a couple of misfires three or four laps before
I came in,' he said, his best poker face to the fore. 'Everyone
on the team is working hard and the guys have been doing
a super job all summer, so it is a big shame that we are
having problems beyond our control. But I am not deflated,
not for an instant, and once our luck changes, I have no
doubt that we will start winning races.'

At that juncture, this sounded akin to another *Blackadder*
character, General Sir Anthony Cecil Hogmanay Melchett,
who once remarked: 'If nothing else works, a total pig-

headed unwillingness to look facts in the face will see us through.' But, just when it looked as if Dario's aspirations were diminishing, he was as good as his word in rebounding from his difficulties to seize his first triumph of the season with a commanding display at the Molson Indy in Toronto, where he led for the entire 95 laps of the tussle and was in his own private bubble of ascendancy, crossing the finish line more than two and a half seconds ahead of Tracy. It was an ideal demonstration of how results can be trans- formed, almost with the clicking of a switch, and also provided ample examples of Franchitti's skill, such as when he overtook de Ferran on the opening lap and was never surpassed thereafter. The latter was despatched to the back of the field for making contact with a tyre in Dario's pit box, but, in this instance, there were to be no twists or belated glitches for the Team Kool Green associates, who were further heartened to learn that Montoya had been involved in a shunt with Michel Jourdain Jnr and had been left pointless, discomfited and irate in the process. Suddenly, the whole destiny of the title was up in the air again and Franchitti was understandably elated as he assessed the contest and where it left him. 'The start was a little bit of a worry, because somebody hit me. I don't know who it was, but it was a bit tight in the first corner and I had to keep my head down and forge ahead. But once I managed to get past Gil, the car was awesome all afternoon and it was the best out there, I don't think anybody could argue with that. We did as competitive lap times as we needed to do. On the pit stops, the TKG guys did a fantastic job, so what more can you ask for? It means a lot to win here, and it is such a terrific crowd, because they always give me so much support. To finally win the race in front of them is pretty awesome and when your team-mate is second, the entire organisation can enjoy the moment. That is why we are here racing and why people such as myself love this sport and, hopefully, if we can maintain this form, we might be showing the Ganassi boys around the track pretty soon.'

What could not be denied was the twisty nature of the championship and the trend continued with another exhilarating package of thrills when the circus rolled into Michigan for the 250-lap US 500. Unfortunately, from Franchitti's point of view, he was relegated to bit-part status while the day's main focus of attention revolved around a mesmerising battle between Tony Kanaan, Montoya and Andretti, with the latter duo engaged in an early struggle for supremacy which resembled the intensity of the chariot duel between Charlton Heston and Stephen Boyd in *Ben Hur*. The Colombian had enjoyed a superb start, forcing his way into the lead, but for the next ten laps, Andretti hung tenaciously to his gearbox and circuit after circuit or the pair sped through corners side by side with the lead changing hands at a bewildering rate. 'It was a nightmare,' said Montoya later, with a chuckle which suggested that he had loved every moment of it. 'Even if you are faster, you pass someone, then they pass you back, you pass them again, and they do the same to you, and you are concentrating so much on one person that you hardly notice when another competitor is doing his own thing somewhere else.'

As the race advanced, Montoya gained the upper hand and established a lead which he held until the third set of pit stops. But his relative lack of experience cost him dearly, when he showed hesitation in traffic, and his problems mounted when he lost his rear brakes halfway through the event, which meant that when he came into the pits for his penultimate stop, he was shocked when he couldn't stop his car as quickly as he had envisaged and overshot the pit area. His afternoon was deteriorating. Further back in the pack, Franchitti was suffering a lacklustre showing, and emerged as second best to Paul Tracy, in a duel between the pair which led to several near-collisions with walls, their joust demonstrating that neither was interested in tactical strategies.

Amidst all this pulsating activity, Kanaan stayed as calm as he could, and profited on the mistakes of others. Montoya lost six positions in each of his last two pit stops and, but for his brake difficulties, would surely have gained maximum points, because he still fought back strongly and challenged Kanaan on the final lap, before the Brazilian eventually wrapped up his first CART victory in dramatic circumstances and basked in his success, mindful of how he had been caught up in so many crashes in the previous rounds. Behind him and Montoya came Tracy, Andretti and Franchitti, a state of affairs which saw the title leader increase his advantage over Dario to 129-116. Nevertheless, the Scot remained convinced he could still retrieve and surpass that deficit and, if anything, was as bullish in the wake of a sub-par display as he had been exuberant in Toronto. Yet, as he explained to me, that was one of the great motivations of his vocation; the task of squaring the circle between insuperability and inability in a car from one week to another. 'You have to be phlegmatic about these things, but occasionally it can be as frustrating as hell, and there doesn't seem to be a lot of logic to what is going on. I suppose it boils down to one of the reasons why I am fascinated by this form of racing and why Formula One sometimes appears a bit boring to me, by comparison. Let's face it, in F1, the best two or three cars are invariably the ones whose drivers end up on the podium, and although I am not taking anything away from the skill levels involved, it isn't as exciting or as unpredictable as in this CART scene, where any one of eight or nine different drivers can come out of the blocks and win on any given weekend. It proves how much strength in depth there is in this competition, and one of the things you can guarantee is that if you ever think you have all the answers, then something will happen to make you realise that you don't. You have to get used to that or you will drive yourself nuts.'

It was an admirable approach to tackling life's slings and arrows, but there again, Franchitti had been forced to eschew any complacency during the course of his stop-start career and he would encounter more of the same in the years ahead. Yet, as if to accentuate his belief in the ephemeral nature of most sporting problems, Dario sealed his second win in three CART races with a stunning success in the Tenneco Automotive Grand Prix of Detroit at the Raceway on Belle Isle (a really snappy title for the event, eh?) on August 8 and suddenly leapt ahead of Montoya in the Fedex Championship Series standings, where, only few weeks earlier, his title bid had seemed fated to founder in mishaps. Having trailed 130–116 in advance of the race, he established a 136–131 lead, and nobody could begrudge him his tangible delight in the post-race environs, where, probably for the first time since his induction to American motor sport, Dario was becoming something of a celebrity. Certainly, he merited praise for the fashion in which he recovered from a poorish start to his weekend, with Montoya qualifying pole, and subsequently leading for 58 of the 71 laps, but a breakdown in communication between him and his pit crew proved very costly and while the Ganassi gang flapped, floundered and faffed around, Franchitti retrieved a 15-second deficit, and transformed that into a 10-second cushion as his main opponent slipped back to eighth place – which was only the prelude to his day going from bad to worse in the closing stages. Dario, by comparison, was rock-solid in cementing his position, whereas Montoya, quick but impetuous as ever, launched a charge back towards the front, but met with a series of minor calamities in the process. On lap 62, he sought to overtake Roberto Moreno, but merely succeeded in making contact with him. Then, some four laps later, he was in seventh place when a caution came out, following a four-car incident. Finally, Helio Castroneves shunted into his fellow South American, and that was the end of Montoya's odyssey.

In the midst of this torrent of thrills and spills, Franchitti was master and commander, and was not required to fend off any sustained challenge from Paul Tracy in the last 13 laps, prior to taking the checkered flag. In doing so, he affirmed his superiority on the street circuits which comprised a significant part of the CART schedule. Indeed, if every event had been staged in such circumstances, Franchitti would have been on as many podia as Michael Schumacher in F1, but he was just happy to have regained the initiative, considering how far he had been off the pace at the start of the championship. 'It was a very interesting day, although I don't imagine it was particularly the nicest race to watch. The way the day went, I got past Gil [de Ferran] at the start, then Paul began to pull away, but, honestly, it was Juan's to lose today, and I don't know what happened with his team. The race turned for us on the second pit stop. We chose to come in, as most of the field did, and when we went back out again, we started saving fuel like crazy. It's a nice feeling when you are leading and the yellow comes out, but you don't really want to cross the finish line going at 20mph [as a consequence of the accidents which had occurred elsewhere on the circuit]. But, hey, in the grand scheme, it is terrific to have a one-two finish, and with Greg [Moore] being up there on the podium as well, I suppose that it couldn't really have gone much better for us than it did.'

The relationship between Franchitti and Moore went

beyond mutual respect and converged into genuine comrade-ship. The Scot was 26, the Canadian 23, but they shared a reverence for the history and traditions of their sport and had no time for the brash, or the self-aggrandising bullshit, which poured forth from several of the other drivers. Dario's regard for his younger rival was heartfelt and that sentiment was returned by Moore, as he explained in his post-race observations. 'My team did a tremendous job for me all weekend, and I came in for my first pit stop in eighth and came out fourth which is a testament to my crew and the skill of these guys. Had we seen a green finish, I don't know how Dario and Paul would have been on fuel – we would have made it to the end of the race, probably by the skin of our teeth, but I don't know if Dario and Paul would have made it. But third place, considering the bad string of luck we have suffered over the last few races, is good for the team and you can't get upset when you see somebody like Dario gaining the benefit for all the hard work he has put in. All in all, it was a good result for us all and if I can't win the title this year, then I hope that Dario does.'

None the less, it was impossible to denigrate the manner in which Montoya had risen to the challenge in his debut CART campaign, and regardless of whatever setbacks he encountered, he possessed a blistering speed and an equal amount of self-confidence. By mid-August, when the competition moved to Lexington in the Miller Lite 200 in Ohio, he could have been forgiven for starting to succumb to the pressure which was being heaped on him by Franchitti, but it was characteristic of the man and his methods that his response was to record a thoroughly convincing victory – his fifth of the season – as the title contest took another turn. At the outset, such a result might have looked improbable, considering how Dario amassed a five-second lead in the early stages, with Tracy the nearest to him at that period, but the first round of pit stops proved instrumental in boosting Montoya, who gained five positions on the track, as he signalled his intention to blow away anybody who stood in his path. He was assisted when Franchitti was blighted by a tyre problem, which forced him to pit early, and Tracy was unable to stem the Colombian tide, with Montoya executing an audacious outside move to storm past the Team Kool Green driver. 'When he passed me, he got a good run on me going into the corner, so I tried to protect the line and force him to go wide, but Juan went in a little deeper than I had anticipated and you have to give credit to him for that,' said an admiring Tracy afterwards. 'They ought to put "Superman" on his car, because what he achieved out there this afternoon was more than special. It was fantastic.'

Franchitti had the consolation of securing third spot, and still led the title, albeit by one solitary point, but he was intelligent enough to appreciate the magnitude of Montoya's exploits and applaud how he had become the first rookie to win five events in a season since Nigel Mansell in 1993. But Dario also recognised that his vehicle was performing in fits and starts and that was a patent source of anxiety. 'Paul would have let me by, but I couldn't get close enough and we were both running at the same pace, so we just had to settle with what we got,' he said with as stoical an air as he could muster.

Yet, if he could sense Montoya breathing down his neck, the situation worsened the following week when the South American maestro swept to another triumph in Chicago, which allowed him to regain the CART lead, by four points, from his rival. The proceedings reflected the fashion in which butterflies were beginning to set in as summer started to fade towards the end of August, but what was most galling for Dario was the fact that this was a far from comfortable event for Montoya and yet he still retained his composure and orchestrated sufficient momentum to keep his eye on the prize.

On reflection, that was one of the facets of Montoya's personality which enabled him to prosper in his new surroundings, namely, the aptitude for transcending adversity and turning it to his advantage. 'Most of the weekend was really bad,' he said. 'We couldn't get the car working the way that we wanted it and last night we stayed here until pretty late and all of my guys tried to figure out what was going on with the car.' Montoya's approach confirmed the view that if genius truly is an infinite capacity for taking pains, then he was Stephen bloody Hawking. 'I went out in the morning warm-up and had a little bit of understeer, yet it was lot less problematic than it had been 24 hours earlier. But I still didn't feel that my confident about my chances. Just goes to show . . .'

It may have been an inauspicious preparation, but once the action commenced, that scarcely seemed to concern Montoya. Early in the proceedings, he decided he was not going to languish in everybody else's slipstream; he would either thrust himself into contention or take his vehicle straight to the knacker's yard. 'When the race started, initially I was a bit unsure what to do, but then I thought to myself that being aggressive was the best policy: I moved quite quickly until I was behind [Helio] Castroneves, then after I went past him, the car was flying and that was it,' he proclaimed. 'I wasn't really a contender until just before the race. But that was fantastic work from the guys.'

Franchitti was hardly inclined to join in the euphoric revelry. On the plus side, he finished second and duly recorded his fourth podium berth in the space of five events. But, on the debit sheet, he had stayed close to Montoya throughout the proceedings, had snapped at his heels, in best terrier style, and had reduced the gap to a mere two-tenths of a second with the denouement beckoning, without ever quite having the juice or, perhaps, the inner conviction to transcend his handling problems and gain a precious victory. Even now, from such a distance, Dario's skill, his decency and decorum were all valuable traits in his armoury, but when it boiled down to being nasty, to slipping occasionally into Dick Dastardly territory, he struck one as being too civilised for his own good.

Indeed, even Franchitti's assessment of the events at Cicero sounded more like oratory than old-fashioned anger. 'I was fighting an oversteer going into the corner on the brakes. There was a little understeering through the middle and an oversteer on exit. I could see that he [Montoya] was oversteering coming out, leaving some nice black lines on occasion. I was simply trying to get as close as I could to him into the corner to get a run on him at exit. I was just waiting for one small mistake in traffic, just one guy to hold him up in the wrong place and then I would pounce on him. [Roberto] Moreno came up, who had pitted out of sequence, and he came steaming down the inside and got between us, which wasn't remotely helpful to me. He spoiled my race, but I think Juan was pretty happy with what happened. On sheer speed, it wouldn't have been easy for me to get past Juan, but in traffic, on these tracks, you only wait for one mistake and that is all it takes. The bottom line is that if somebody had blocked him or had held him up, I would have been able to get a slingshot and move past him. But I guess I can't let it worry me too much. We are still very much in the title fight and we have to keep plugging away.'

All the same, the force was with JP and, as if to illustrate the size of the task in front of Franchitti, his nemesis seized a third consecutive success on his next assignment in Vancouver, where his pre-race plans were as smooth as they had been unsatisfactory in the previous event – the only similarity was the commitment with which Montoya sprinted to his seventh win of the campaign and carved out what began to forge a potentially decisive advantage in the CART stakes. The vagaries of the climate, mechanical problems, technical naïveté . . . nothing seemed to faze the youngster, whose triumph allowed him to build up a 23-point cushion over Franchitti, whose afternoon was once again in stark contrast to the man he was seeking to overhaul. In bare statistically terms, Montoya led for 73 of the 74 laps en route to his objective and a comfortable checkered flag, nearly eight seconds in front of Patrick Carpentier. He wasn't bothered in the slightest by the intervention of the elements, which transformed the race into a timed two-hour affair, in accordance with the championship regulations, and only surrendered his lead – for a solitary lap – to Paul Tracy, before resuming normal service.

None of which is to traduce the effort of Franchitti, who proved his worth as a tough hombre and put his foot on the throttle with a red-blooded intensity which showed that he was no slouch, even if the conditions were not conducive to miracles. He swept beyond Tracy on lap 51 and immediately embarked in hot pursuit of Montoya, to such positive effect that he began to put pressure on his opponent after a restart on lap 59. But sadly, at the precise moment when it seemed he might engineer a thrilling recovery, and as he attempted to get underneath Montoya in Turn 4, he spun out and made slight contact with the Colombian, as the precursor to crashing into the tyre barrier. JP was able to carry on, unhindered by the collision, but Dario's car had sustained heavy rear-wing damage and although this was repaired, amidst a frantic pit stop, his last-gasp exertions to claw back as much time as he could were rewarded with nothing better than tenth place and a modest haul of three points, in comparison to the 22 which were accrued by Montoya.

For some people, this was enough to crown the latter as champion, even though there was plenty of time remaining for matters to change – as indeed materialised. But some of the triumphalist nonsense which appeared in the Colombian press was not so much premature as stupid, in an event where accidents and danger are an inevitable part of the equation and where the risk of injury or fatality is never far from centre stage. If anybody required reminding of that queasy truism, they were brought back to reality in the next race of the CART series at Laguna Seca in California, where Bryan Herta captured victory, Montoya struggled to eighth and Franchitti didn't finish the event at all. But somehow, none of that was very important once the news filtered through on the Saturday afternoon that the rookie driver Gonzalo Rodriguez had been killed in a dreadful accident during the practice session. 'What can you say?' asked Max Papis, who secured his first podium, but confirmed he had been left feeling numb with shock. 'Where you end up in the standings and how many points you score just isn't that important when a guy loses his life out there. It is just a very sad weekend for all of us here.'

The traditional spraying of champagne was cancelled and silent prayers were uttered for the fallen one. Yet, it was almost of a portent of what lay ahead that Franchitti's race should have climaxed after an incident with Greg Moore of all people. While attempting a passing movement at the entrance to Turn 2, Dario collided with his friend, sending the Scot's car into the gravel pit and terminating his participation. For his part, Moore strove to continue, only to be frustrated as his transmission failed in the next lap.

It was a miserable end to a sorrowful experience. But there was worse, much worse, in store for Franchitti and Moore, as the campaign advanced towards its finale.

5

Into A Dark Place

If there was one quality which had always defined Dario Franchitti, it lay in his ability to conform to the ideal image of the boy next door. When we met at a garage in Edinburgh at the beginning of his career, he lolloped into the forecourt with the easy charm and excited countenance of a lad who had just been offered his first car on turning 18. A decade later, he was similarly lacking in pretensions upon walking past the reception at the Scotsman Publications' new offices on Holyrood Road in Edinburgh and managed the rare feat of eliciting laughs and whimsy from a group of employees, the majority of whom were apprehensive about the spectre of job losses and looming salary cuts.

Yet, as Dario steeled himself for the final three events in the 1999 Fedex CART Championship, even this normally most level-headed of individuals admitted that the multifarious ingredients of a roller-coaster season had left him feeling under pressure. No Icarus, inclined to soar too close to the sun, nor burdened with a Cassandra disposition, which eternally made him fear the worst, Franchitti was all the same more nervous than when we had previously conversed. That was understandable in the circumstances, given how his conflict with Juan Pablo Montoya had developed into a searing war of attrition, which appeared to be slipping away from the Scot, who arrived in Houston, Texas, a daunting 28 points behind his Ganassi rival. 'In some respects, it has been fantastic and in others, frustrating, and sometimes these two things have come together in the same race, but I have maintained all year that we have been very close to reaching our potential on a consistent basis and now we have to take the next step up and do our best to collect the maximum amount of points in the remaining races,' said Franchitti, whose title aspirations depended on both his success and a collapse from Montoya. 'You have to give credit to Juan, because he has come into the series and has won seven races and you can't achieve that without having a lot of ability. But, equally, we have put some strong sequences of results together and I reckon that we can do that again from now on.'

However, the tone of much of the Stateside coverage reflected the American writers' view on the most likely scenario, and much of that pro-Montoya reporting echoed a widespread opinion that he was receiving preferential treatment from his employers, whereas Franchitti and Paul Tracy had kept matters entirely above board when a few team orders in Dario's favour might have transformed the entire picture. As somebody who deprecated the fashion in which David Coulthard slowed down on the final lap of the Australian Grand Prix in Melbourne in 1998, permitting his McLaren team-mate, Mika Hakkinen, to secure a prearranged and thoroughly undeserved victory, I have always clung to the notion that real sport shouldn't have any truck with these sort of nefarious pacts. And yet, by the conclusion of the CART action in Houston, there was another part of me which felt that the Team Kool Green had just blown their prospects by being excessively honest.

Arguably, of course, they were simply being true to their principles and Tracy had performed sufficiently well throughout the 1999 series to feel that he was entitled to capitalise on his success, as he wound up in front of Franchitti. For starters, he had seized the lead when Montoya crashed out of contention, and subsequently served up a master class in the art of race strategy and fuel conservation which might have satisfied Al Gore. But, regardless of his skill, the inconvenient truth for the organisation was that Tracy had no chance of winning the title, in which light it would have benefited Franchitti a lot more to have taken the checkered flag. And, besides, this wasn't a similar scenario to that of the aforementioned 'After You, Claude' routine from Coulthard, which occurred in the very first race of the 1998 F1 season.

But, whatever the merits or otherwise of the TKG tactics, Barry Green had resolved that he was not interested in telling Tracy to let Franchitti pass him and the team had ample time to weigh up the consequences of this decision in the future. Perhaps they were sending out a discreet message to Dario that he would have to up the stakes the following season to gain extra privileges. Or maybe Tracy's words testified to his feeling that, after suffering problems at the Houston circuit in previous encounters, he was yielding to nobody, not even his colleague. 'I was dominant out there. I had the best car, I had the best tyres from qualifying, the set that I rubbed the wall with on the first day. They were fresh and it was like a "Sunday drive" out there. We just ran away from everybody else in the field and, as far as I am concerned, the win was never a problem for us.'

When questioned by the media as to whether they knew Barry Green had briefly considered asking Paul to step aside in order to gain more championship points, both of the Team Kool Green drivers denied they had heard the subject being discussed on their radios, which, at least to an outsider, sounds strangely unconvincing. Nor was the quality of the debate heightened when Tracy followed his answer up by declaring that if he had heard any such instructions being issued, his radio 'would have developed a very bad case of static'. But, of course, it is easy to be wise with hindsight and Franchitti, whether or not he was inwardly seething, appeared unconcerned by the subject. 'I would like to thank the guy upstairs. We were struggling at the beginning and I had a car which I couldn't drive. Every time I turned right, it would snap back to the left because of the oversteer and it was very difficult,' said Franchitti. 'That first yellow (following Montoya's crash), was very timely and it definitely helped me to pull things together. But this was Paul's day, there was never an issue about him winning, he deserved his victory, he was over ten seconds ahead at the end of the race and good luck to him.'

The final words should probably go to Barry Green, if only because he articulated a fear which came to be remarkably prescient as the dust settled on the Texan one-two. 'Paul drove a tremendous race and got fantastic mileage there at the end. *Now I just hope we don't miss the championship by four points* [my italics]. With Michael [Andretti] on Dario's tail, I had to go with my instincts and I am happy with that. It was a great team effort from the guys, it was brilliant to be involved in it and the championship is still very much alive. Another one-two would be just wonderful.'

The upshot of all this honest brokering was that Montoya's CART lead had been reduced from 29 to 13, as the prelude to the competitors embarking on the gruelling trip to Australia. One American journalist sought to explain the various permutations, but might have been better leaving the vision thing to Mr Magoo. 'If Montoya takes pole, leads the most laps and wins the Surfer's Paradise race two weeks from now, and Franchitti finishes fourth or worse, then the Colombian will become the first rookie since Nigel Mansell to win the title.' As might have been envisaged, nothing was ever going to be that elementary in this most convoluted of campaigns. And especially not, considering how Dario was suddenly reinvigorated with lashings of self-belief and optimism.

In any case, whatever problems he might have experienced on certain tracks, Dario was a virtuoso performer on street circuits, and as he touched down in the Gold Coast, there was a warm welcome from a mass of spectators, many of whom boasted Scottish or Italian ancestry, and were rooting for the man with a sprinkling of both cultures in his psyche. During the past decade, Indycar's administrators have done their best to extend interest in the sport outwith North America, and Franchitti's battle with Montoya was exactly the kind of no-holds-barred contest which might have been specially designed to eradicate apathy and generate a crescendo of noise, even in a country which rarely looked beyond cricket, rugby league and Aussie Rules. However, that premise depended on the duo reprising the tumultuous nip and tuck which had typified their season-long fight. In the event, there was no repeat – for the simple reason that Dario destroyed his opponent with one of the most convincing displays it would be possible to imagine, both wiping the floor with Montoya and regaining pole position in the CART title pursuit at the end of an imperious exhibition of his powers. In advance, the weather forecast had hinted at rain, but the heavy cloud cover lifted in time for the start, whereupon Franchitti seized the lead and never really threatened to relinquish it for the remainder of the afternoon.

Away from the Team Kool Green man, there were incidents a-plenty. Paul Tracy was black-flagged for passing

Bryan Herta before the start/finish line; Gil de Ferran quickly locked his tyres and slid into a wall, which forced him to make a premature retirement; Christian Fittipaldi bowed out with an oil fire at the rear of his vehicle: Michel Jourdain Jnr and Patrick Carpentier's cars made contact, with the latter requiring help from the safety officials to get started again . . . but you can probably guess at the pandemonium which had erupted amongst some of the less experienced street drivers. On lap 35, Mark Blundell's race was abruptly curtailed, following a spin with Shigeaki Hattori, and shortly thereafter, Jimmy Vasser had to retire with plumes of smoke emanating from his vehicle, before Greg Moore was forced out with electrical problems. Then, in what seemed to be one of the most significant developments of the whole season, Montoya, who was struggling badly to keep pace with Franchitti, betrayed his unfamiliarity with competing on these kind of circuits and understeered into the wall at Turn 9 on lap 49, which ended his involvement and handed Dario a fantastic opportunity to win.

It was not an opening he had any intention of squandering and, as the race raged on, Franchitti was an oasis of calmness, combining efficiency and expertise without having to contemplate any undue risks, in opening up a lead of over three seconds on Max Papis, Adrien Fernandez and Herta. None of them was remotely capable of catching him and as the Scot took the checkered flag, to a standing ovation from thousands of the crowd, the situation had altered dramatically in his championship bid. Suddenly, with 20 points for the win, another for securing pole, and yet another for leading the most laps, he had accelerated to 209 points in the table, nine in front of Montoya, who had derived about as much joy from his visit to Australia as England's Ashes captains in the 1990s. With one event left, in Fontana on October 31, Dario seemed to have peaked at the right time.

'From the start of the race, we got a jump on Bryan Herta. We were fairly comfortable and we managed to build a consistent gap. The first pit stop took a little longer than I would have liked, but after it settled down, there was a yellow a couple of laps after that, which was very lucky, because if that had happened the lap after we pitted, then we would have been in real trouble,' said Franchitti, as usual predisposed to downplay his own abilities. 'When we came back out, Montoya was behind me, Bryan had been put back, and I thought to myself: "Everyone else is falling by the wayside". Montoya wasn't that quick either, but he was making up ground for no other reason than that other drivers were falling out of the race. After that, I just had to get on with it, focus on my own race and tactics and save fuel and not make any mistakes. But then, Kim Green came over the radio and told me there was a local yellow, at whatever lap it was, and that Montoya had just gone out of the race. I went: "Okay, this is perfect, this is what we were looking for, we are looking at 22 points and he has none, but now we can't afford any mistakes", and we had to stay alert and avoid relaxing, because we have all seen how many things have happened this season. After that, when I was sitting behind Jan Magnussen, it was kind of interesting, because I have raced against Jan since I was 14, in karts, and he was my team-mate for three years, so I knew that if I made a move on him, he would see me and give me the appropriate room, so that worked out fine. It was a terrific day, all round.'

The bubbly expression on his face and the collective joie de vivre of the Team Kool Green ensemble reflected the conviction that, although nothing could be taken for granted, the pressure and expectations had all been transplanted to their Ganassi counterparts and Montoya in particular, who must have envisaged that winning seven of the 19 races would have permitted him some clear water in the drivers' championship. However, what should have been a titanic struggle for supremacy at the California Speedway in Fontana on the last day of October was destined to be remembered not for the quality of the action, or even an anti-climactic technical glitch bedevilling one of the contenders, but for something else altogether. It was something which extended beyond the realm of mere motoring trivia and touched the hearts of all the CART participants with such a resonance that few championships in any sport can ever have been won and lost with so little celebration or commiseration on either side of the divide.

Thus it was that even *motorsport.com*, a magnificently detailed website, which can normally be relied upon to cover every cough, grunt and fart from the pit and paddock, responded to the proceedings with the tristesse which fitted the occasion. 'Adrian Fernandez won the race and Juan Montoya captured the championship today. But the celebrations were replaced by tears as the sport lost Greg Moore, who died in a car accident on lap 10 of the 500-mile race,' said the report. 'Moore was fatally injured in an incident when his car lost control at the exit of Turn 2, slamming into an inside retaining wall. The impact of this sent the car tumbling across the apron grass, causing extensive damage to the vehicle, but of far greater significance, Moore was airlifted to Loma Linda Medical Facility where efforts to resuscitate him were unsuccessful.'

It was as if a candle had been snuffed out and the stunned, lachrymose faces of hard-bitten competitors converging in shared grief reflected both the disbelief with which they heard the news, and also the immense affection in which Moore was held within their ranks. Franchitti, for instance, knew something was wrong long before his own race had concluded, but was still shocked to the core when his father,

George, haltingly broke the news to his son, at which point any disappointment Dario might have been harbouring was replaced with a broader expression of humanity. According to somebody within the CART sphere, tears were shed, copiously, publicly, by distraught young men for the rest of the evening. The more experienced stalwarts, for whom this wasn't the first or even tenth fatality in their vocation, sought to issue tributes which summed up their feelings and even attempted to make sense of what couldn't be rationalised. But Dario, for a while, was inconsolable and we are not speaking here of a few days or even a few weeks of him – dread phrase – 'coming to terms' with the loss. Indeed, three years later, when he won a race in Canada, he dedicated the victory to the memory of Greg Moore and the tremble in his lips provided a reminder that some awful things are never forgotten.

Nor was there anything but shock and raw grief in the next few days, so much so that even though Moore's family asked the end-of-season CART presentation ceremony to proceed as planned, the only subject which seemed to matter to the audience was the young fellow who had just died. 'The loss of Greg is a hard thing to try and stomach, because he had more talent in his little pinkie than most guys in their whole bodies,' said Paul Tracy of his compatriot, who had suffered a hand injury in the build-up to the race in Fontana and only competed after an eleventh-hour decision. As for Montoya, all the plaudits he had earned for a sensational debut season were disfigured and diminished. 'I would give up this whole title just to have Greg back, because he was one hell of a great guy and he lit up the whole sport with his attitude, his ability and his sheer enthusiasm for what he was doing,' declared the Colombian. 'It is very difficult to take in that he has been killed, and he didn't deserve to die. You never think that anything like this will happen to anybody such as Greg who was such a natural in the car and yet here we are today lamenting another casualty. You just want to go as quick as you can, that was Greg's philosophy, and he had faith in his skills and loved what he was doing. Maybe that is the only consolation from this tragedy, but it doesn't help anybody much just now.'

As for Franchitti, who was closer to Moore than anybody, the events in Fontana had not only left him shattered, but forced him to think back to the number of other legends of the sport who had sparkled in their vocation and then perished in their pomp. 'I lost one of the best friends I ever had in Greg. In the last couple of years, ever since I got to know him, we shared a tremendous amount of good times together. He was the guy I competed with hardest on the track and he was the guy that I had the most fun with away from the circuit. The guy was going to be a champion, many, many times over and I still have to pinch myself to remember that he is never going to walk through the door again with the words: "How are you doing?" With what has happened, nothing else matters. When you see his record and you know how good he was, in those Penske Hondas and subsequently in the IRL, I shudder to think what would have happened. He would have made the rest of us look stupid at times. Car control, overtaking, courage, charisma . . . he had the lot, and there is a huge amount of sadness at the moment.'

And yet, as Dario reflected on his past, there was also the death of maestri such as Jim Clark and Gilles Villeneuve to recall, even before one turned to the sickening weekend in F1 in May 1994 at Imola, where Roland Ratzenberger and Ayrton Senna died on the Saturday and Sunday. 'When Jackie [Stewart] talks about Jimmy, he is still in awe and for Jackie to be like that, the guy must have been absolutely amazing. In my new house, one of the bedrooms is the Jim Clark Room. All the tiles in the bedroom are the blue from his helmet and I spent months tracking them down. They are just so cool.

'You sometimes think back to the guys who are no longer with us and it reminds you that risks are part of this business. The other day, I was thinking about Gilles Villeneuve and I actually asked myself: "Was Gilles really as good as I remember?" So I logged on to the YouTube site and watched some stuff and the guy drove an F1 vehicle as if it was a bloody rally car. How did he do it? It was amazing – what a fantastic gift he had.'

Such reminiscences explain Franchitti's fascination with the evolution of motor racing in all its diverse forms, but also underlined how his values and priorities were far removed from those sports stars cursed with the belief that they are owed a living and that the world revolves around their activities. On the contrary, Dario grew ever closer to Ashley and the pair were engaged at the end of 1999, even though there was no public announcement until April 2000. The Franchitti family had swiftly taken their son's girlfriend to their hearts, not simply because she was home-spun, down-to-earth and idealistic – some of the same qualities which were shared by Dario – but through the realisation that the couple were so happy together and enjoyed a special bond that, despite only having known each other for less than a year, they could finish the other's sentences, swapped repartee with a machine-gun-like rapidity and were clearly so right for one another.

Obviously, their careers diverged in contrasting directions, but the pair shared a love for the bucolic life, whether hiking, exploring the countryside, both in Scotland and the United States, and taking care of the dogs, cats and chickens with which they shared their lives at home in Tennessee. 'We have what is most important,' said Judd, in one of the few conversations she had about the relationship. 'We are very comfortable together in the quiet moments.' As for the perils and pitfalls involved in his profession, which had been accentuated by the demise of Greg Moore, Judd was equally pragmatic. 'I think that fear is a choice and it is one I have chosen not to make. I mean, I could be wound up about it every time that he races or I could not. And I'm not.' The couple had often to check their diaries to arrange meetings, given his hectic itinerary and her cinematic appearances, which often necessitated late-night and early-morning shooting sessions in big-city locations. But, once more, she had a practical approach to the problems. 'I don't want to slag New York, say. It's a very special place. You can get Indian food at 3am. But personally, I don't want Indian food at 3am. I want to go for a walk in my nightgown, in peace and quiet. I'm just not an urban person and neither is Dario.'

After the thrilling tussle for the CART crown in 1999, Dario experienced an underwhelming campaign in the following year when a heavy crash in pre-season training ruined his prospects of repeating his heroics, and although he bounced back with five top-five finishes, two pole positions and a hat-trick of podium berths, he couldn't conjure up a single victory. Matters improved considerably in 2001 when he triumphed in Cleveland and ended up fourth in the championship standings. Yet the most important chapter in the latter year was undoubtedly his wedding to Ashley at Skibo Castle, near Dornoch in Scotland, in December, where he was as unassuming as ever in letting his wife take centre stage.

It was, typically, for a duo who relished their privacy, the antithesis of the *Hello!*-style nuptials, where small forests are demolished to make room for page after page of pictures of the Beckhams or the Rooneys or the union of Madonna and Guy Ritchie. Indeed, in the build-up to the ceremony on December 12, Judd mapped out her plans in a chamber she dubbed the 'war room', and even hung a picture of Winston Churchill on the wall to stiffen her resolve that there would be no paparazzi, no unwanted guests and certainly no intrusive tabloid journalists, prepared to sift through the garbage in pursuit of profitable tittle-tattle. Earlier that year, Franchitti had told me that he couldn't understand the British obsession with gossip, rumour and innuendo and revealed that he simply couldn't contemplate a similar existence to that of David and Victoria Beckham. 'It must become unbearable at times. Sure, we are in the public eye and we are well rewarded for what we do, but that doesn't and never will mean that we are public property on a 24/7 basis,' he said, with an unusual frisson in his voice. In which light, it was understandable that the wedding was off-limits to all but the twosome's families and a few select friends.

Predictably, of course, none of this prevented an abundance of lurid reports on both sides of the Atlantic. 'Practically, everything in the papers was completely untrue, and we don't even know most of the people the papers said we invited,' said Judd. 'One journalist decided that Sandra Bullock [the star of such films as *Speed*, *The Net* and *While You Were Sleeping*) and I were best friends and that she was my maid of honour, but the latter part was nonsense. I recently e-mailed her and said: "You know I got married." And she replied: "Yeah, I know. People keep asking me about it. I just tell them that I was too drunk to remember anything and that seems to do the trick."'

What little that emerged that *was* true demonstrated that the bride and groom preferred substance and style over ostentation and arriviste archness. Dario, Ashley, and their parents, brothers and sisters, such as George, Marina, Marino and Carla Franchitti and Naomi and Wynonna Judd, spent the days leading up to the ceremony horse-riding, playing golf, admiring the scenery, dining in the opulent reception rooms and enjoyed a traditional ceilidh, complete with pipers and national costume. As for the wedding itself, the most appealing aspect was the child-like wonder in both of their faces as the big day beckoned. 'It was amazing from the moment we first showed up at the castle – just knowing that in a few days, we were going to be married,' enthused Dario, whilst the loquacious Ashley tripped herself up in a bundle of good-golly-gosh. 'It is unbelievable, incredible. Being married just goes to beyond anything that I can't even begin to describe. Words fail me. I over-rely on superlatives, but how do you express . . . ?'

It was a world away from the sadness which engulfed them after Greg's death. But they had to respond to a series of new challenges once the honeymoon was over.

6

SNAPSHOTS OF AN INVISIBLE MAN

Dario Franchitti was never interested in publicity for the sake of it. As has already been explained, his abiding love for motor-sport was his main motivation and if that required him to stride into the PR gaze from time to time, he accepted the responsibility with a few jokes, a self-deprecating response to his privileged lifestyle, and a polite handshake with those who met and interviewed him on any kind of regular basis. If it occasionally appeared that he was an anonymous figure on the IndyCar beat, that didn't worry him unduly. Indeed, there were many instances where he seemed to thrive in the anonymity, whether in being able to stroll down the thoroughfares of Scotland's major cities without being recognised or slipping in and out of Celtic Park after watching his favourite football team strut their stuff. Such invisibility was not available to those who plied their trade at Parkhead, as anybody who has ever been seated in the back of a Glasgow taxi will acknowledge. 'Have you heard about this?', 'Do you know about that?', 'I've got a pal who says that we're putting in a bid for Ronaldo, is that true?' . . . these are the sort of inquiries which soon become a tiresome chore for anybody who happens to hail a cab within the vicinity of the Scottish champions' ground. The former Celtic chairman, Fergus McCann, once grew so fed up about being bombarded with questions by cabbies that as soon as he entered a taxi, his first and only words were: 'Just drive.'

If that option had been offered to Franchitti, he would probably have grasped it with both hands at the start of his career, but, as the new millennium came and went, CART entered a state of flux, while administrators from rival organisations argued and bickered over the future direction of the sport, with the kind of petty politicking which makes the actual participants despair. Dario's life became akin to a soap opera in that nothing much happened for months on end, but suddenly, he would feature in a big storyline or take the protagonist's role in a dramatic twist. It was probably asking too much to expect him to maintain the momentum of his 1999 campaign, not least given the tragic fashion in which it concluded, but even so, his life subsequently developed into a frustratingly stop-start affair, interspersed by moments of true passion or emotion, which were worth accentuating without dwelling on the minutiae. In basic terms, he toiled in 2000, rallied a little in 2001, but still entered 2002 with pressure on his shoulders, because he recognised that he had to start gaining regular victories again. By now, it was obvious that there was no passage for him into Formula One, and even if one buys into the PR spin which accompanied his test drive for Jaguar in 2000 – which I don't because I spoke to a couple of the company's officials during a visit to Valencia to interview Eddie Irvine in 2001 and they told me, in matter-of-fact fashion, that Franchitti had been 'well off the pace' – his horizons seemed to be narrowing as he edged closer to 30. In which light, rather than focusing on every single event in which he competed, let us home in on some of the more significant incidents in the life of this strangely invisible man.

Our first port of call is Vancouver, towards the end of July, in 2002, where Dario was striving to secure his maiden victory of the season at the Molson Indy race. In previous outings, he had suffered some misfortune, but had still gathered sufficient points to remain in title contention, but this trip to Canada revolved around more than simply lap times and pit strategies. Two years earlier, Franchitti had been desperate to chase victory, in honour of his fallen comrade, Greg Moore, but had fallen short, but now, he was determined that nothing would stand in his path and, bolstered by a combination of shrewd tactics and good fortune, that objective was attained as Franchitti sped to victory, amidst a barrage of accidents, incidents, cautions, breakdowns and other glitches. By the conclusion, only seven vehicles were still running and three of these had been involved in shunts which had knocked other cars out of the race. It was fast, furious and ultimately free of serious injuries, and for Dario, the triumph was a sweet moment.

It was doubly so, given that he had looked to be out of contention for much of the afternoon. When not under a yellow or red flag, the battle mostly centred around Christian da Matta and Paul Tracy, with Franchitti clinging on to their coat-tails as well he could and benefiting from the labyrinthine regulations which existed on the circuit. For instance, the CART rules insisted that drivers had to pit after a certain number of laps, but Tracy, ever the gambler, staked his bet on the yellow flag coming out before he needed to pit. On other days, in different circumstances, it might have been an inspired ploy, but here, he lost his wager, and blew his chance of winning. From the outset, chaos had fought with pandemonium for supremacy. Fittipaldi, Michael Andretti and Jimmy Vasser locked horns in a way which put the latter and Kenny Brack out of the event. But then Andretti got involved in contact with Tori Takagi and that led to more mayhem, while later in the proceedings, at almost the identical moment, team-mates Fittipaldi and da Matta suffered mechanical failures, which hastened their exits. But the most serious accident occurred when Patrick Carpentier turned sideways at the start of what should have been a short dash to the finish, and the ensuing mass collision saw Alex Tagliani, Bruno Junqueira and Adrian Fernandez spin off the circuit and crash into walls. Amazingly, the trio remained intact, even though Fernandez had to be lifted out of his car and taken to hospital for precautionary X-rays. Some of this carnage was also of the X-rated variety, and the race was understandably red-flagged, but eventually, once the debris and torrent of broken carbon fibre had been cleared up, the event resumed, with a short, sharp five-lap dash to the checkered flag. And guess who emerged with the spoils? Franchitti had thrived by doing what he did best – ducking and diving under the radar, keeping in close communication with his team and reacting best of those in the field to whatever impromptu strategies required to be implemented. It might not have been a contest which he had dominated or even necessarily deserved to win, but Dario had suffered enough problems in the past to recognise that a driver has to capitalise when the breaks fall in his favour, and that is what he did in Vancouver. Paul Tracy, who had led for most of the tussle, was second and Tony Kanaan third, and there were some anxious expressions on the participants' faces as they waited for news of Fernandez. However, in the end, there was nothing serious to report and Franchitti, whose triumph had allowed him to climb up to second place in the championship standings, had the opportunity to pay homage to his team and to Greg Moore in the course of an emotional aftermath.

'It feels awesome [to have won]. But my head is all over the place at the moment with so many things going on in it.

Business first, though. From Team KOOL Green's side of things, it was the perfect weekend, and the race was perfect for Paul and me. I'm sure he would have liked the positions to be reversed, but we played that story a couple of years ago, so now it was my turn. In the race, our pit strategy definitely worked for us today and I just tried not to make any mistakes. And when we pitted and came back out right behind Paul, having done an extra pit stop [to him], I was thinking: "Okay, now we are looking good." Everything went to plan. When da Matta fell out, that was unfortunate for him, but obviously good for us and everything was going great until the red flag came out. I'm glad to hear that Adrian is okay, but that put a whole new spin on the race, going from having a 12-second lead to having Paul right behind me. I just concentrated on making a good restart. I knew that there would be no sort of mad, locking-up manoeuvres from Paul, but if he had got close enough, I am sure that he would have put the pressure on me. And it all worked out for us. Basically, to be standing on the podium with Paul and Tony up here in Vancouver is, yeah, pretty cool.'

As the trio sat together, somebody asked them about Greg, and the memories poured forth. 'Two years ago, I really wanted to win this race as a mark of respect for Greg and just do the business and dedicate it to him. But we screwed up at the last moment in the last pit stop and it wasn't to be. So, today, it is good to finally get the job done. It's a small thing, but it means a lot to me to be able to win up here and I know that if he [Greg] was still here, we would all be out partying tonight . . .'

TONY KANAAN: ' . . . we will be anyway.'

DARIO: 'Yes, we will be; we will just be missing the organiser.'

TONY KANAAN: 'He is organising it, you know that. I think he organised this podium pretty well today.'

DARIO: 'For sure.'

PAUL TRACY: 'I know the feeling that I had when I won here in 2000. I think, to sum it all up, to see [Greg's father] Ric at the podium and see how happy he was, I mean, he was just filled with emotion. And that was great. Really, really great.'

TONY KANAAN: 'Well, what can you say? We have it every year when we come here and it is a tough weekend for us. But it's a lot tougher for Ric and his family. We try to keep it simple and keep remembering him in the best way, which was laughing and having fun. So when we do the partying, we know that he is around. So that's the purpose. We are going to go out and celebrate for him today. It's what he would have wanted.'

By this juncture in his career, Franchitti had risen into the ranks of Britain's highest-paid sports performers, or at least if the figures provided by the annual *Sunday Times* Rich List were to be regarded as gospel. In 2002, David Beckham overtook Prince Naseem Hamed in the standings with estimated earnings of £35m (a figure which has since been completely eclipsed by his move to LA Galaxy), while Hamed, who has subsequently become another in the long line of boxing's busted flushes, picked up £30m. Thereafter, the table continued as follows: Ryan Giggs (£13m), Roy Keane (£13m), Michael Owen (£12m), Andy, sorry, Andrew Cole (£10m), Dario Franchitti (£10m), Tim Henman (£10m) and Steve McMananan (£9m). One English-based newspaper seemed to view this as an indictment of the ridiculous sums of money which were supposedly swilling around in the motoring world, but, if anything the sums quoted merely persuaded this observer to wonder how on earth the likes of Owen, Cole and Henman had managed to gain so much reward from providing so little. By comparison, Franchitti was involved in a genuinely dangerous pursuit, one where he put his life in jeopardy every time he climbed into the cockpit, and where two of his competitors had perished in the 1999 season alone. It's true that Owen had a reputation for going down in the penalty box as if felled by a sniper whenever defenders breathed in his direction, but only a cretin would argue that he was worthy of his salary on the strength of his displays at international level. Yet, while these things are subjective, it should be remembered that, at this point, Tom Cruise was able to demand between £15m and £20m for every film he made, which offers some perspective on the vagaries of the different branches of the entertainment industry.

As for the questions of whether motor racing was as genuine a sport as, say, athletics, or whether it resembled watching paint dry, Franchitti was equitable, but persuasive in his arguments that he couldn't function in his job properly if he indulged in the lifestyle of a Jocky Wilson or Alex Higgins – men whose prowess at their respective sports – darts and snooker – was matched by their ability to down copious quantities of booze. 'When the car is producing something between four and five gs through a corner, you have got to be able to control it, so it is a big misconception that racing drivers aren't fit. Your whole body has to be able to stand these loads, your neck, every part, and when your head is four times its weight all of a sudden, it feels as if somebody is trying to pull it off your shoulder. Which is tough.' Franchitti, not unreasonably, followed that up with the contention that beauty is in the eye of the beholder and that his vocation had more than sufficient fans for him to be able to claim that it was far from being dull, processional or predictable. 'Your mind is processing so many things all of the time that you don't have time to get bored. You are feeling what the car is doing. If you have been in a car when it is sliding around a bit, it feels like that, but you are at the limit of the car. You are focusing on where you are braking, your positioning in the car, how the strategy of the race is running, how the tyres are wearing. You are just constantly processing all the different things that are going on in your small world.'

By this juncture, both Dario and Ashley had grown accustomed to the attention of the paparazzi, whether being pictured together at A-list ceremonies or within their own domains. It would be stretching matters to claim that they enjoyed the more intrusive elements of life as a celebrity couple, but, for most of the time, they acquiesced in the whirr of cameras and provided enough quotable nuggets to offer a snapshot into their private world. The latter quality was very important to them both and even though Ashley accepted that she earned a profitable living from appearing on the big screen, she saw no reason why that should mean she was regarded as public property off the film set.

For one thing, she had to be careful to evade the intrusions and transgressions of stalkers and over-zealous fans and was clearly uneasy with the existence of several websites, mostly run by sad sacks with too much time on their hands, which were devoted to following her career down to the nth degree. More worryingly, one so-called aficionado had broken into her home, prior to her marriage, and although the incident had not caused her any physical harm, it was obvious that the psychological damage was not easily brushed aside. 'Most of the time, I don't find fame scary. I just hope people love the movies, but the fallout which is fame can be a tricky thing, because I do want to have a life,' said Judd, not unreasonably, even while admitting that, occasionally, her and Franchitti's itineraries clashed beyond the point of sanity. While filming *Someone like You* in 2001, she had been scheduled to fly from New York to Los Angeles to watch Dario race, but it was a booking too far. 'I was just exhausted. I got in a limousine on a Saturday night on the way to the airport and it just hit me. I just couldn't do the flight. I was as bummed as a girl could be, but I just couldn't do it. So I had the limo stop in Central Park. It was very late at night and the park was abandoned. And, by this time, it was pouring with rain. I was soaking wet, so the dogs and I just romped through the pond together and it was a great release from all the pressure which I was under.

'But that's how you have to deal with life. As for making movies, it is an inexact science. I'll leave the money decisions to others, because I need inspiration to do the material. It's also about working with people I am simpatico with because it takes a long time to make a movie. But everyday, I think you have a certain amount of feelings that come from an untouchable place. Your feelings are your own responsibility and lead to your choices. It is like that line in a poem: "I am the captain of my own soul." And, as my own captain, I feel as if my life is unfolding the way it should. But you should still be able to go away and do your own thing. You don't talk about your love life or how much money you make or personal matters such as that. You just don't flaunt your stuff.'

This approach was echoed by her husband as the pair sought a bubble of release from the glare of publicity, even if they both acknowledged that, to some extent, their vocations were inextricably linked to the tentacles of a giant PR machine. None the less, when they managed to wriggle out of the spotlight, both the Franchitti and Judd families met on a regular basis in Scotland and the United States and, by all accounts, these trysts were personified by the normal day-to-day things which accompany other, lower-profile unions. Ashley baked corn bread for Dario, he whipped up a decent pasta for her, they watched sport together – he was addicted to football, she was passionate about basketball –

and they enjoyed skipping out on walks, oblivious to the vagaries of the Scottish climate. As of 2002, the duo had flown together on a transatlantic basis enough times for them to be immune to the process, but what was less easy for Dario to come to terms with was the relentless pace of American society, let alone life in the Tinseltown glare.

'I do still get very homesick, and I found the US a bit overpowering at first – everything was so in-your-face and the people over the top, but I eventually got used to it,' said Franchitti, who encountered fewer problems in introducing his parents to his film-star wife. 'No, that's cool – because they know Ashley as Ashley, the girl who will make them breakfast in the morning if they come and stay. She has only missed two races in the last year and although it is difficult when she is filming, she tries her hardest to come to as many of the events as she can. She loves racing now, but before Ashley met me, she most emphatically did not. She saw it as taking TV time away from basketball.'

In short, away from their stellar milieus, they were little different from many people in their position. Dario, for instance, might have been comfortable revving up to 230mph, in the heat of battle, but that sangfroid didn't extend to negotiating the American highway. 'He's a racing driver by profession, but he is also the most nervous passenger in a car when we are just at home,' revealed Judd. 'In fact, I don't get to drive most of the time. And if I do, he is always telling me to slow down. I guess he likes to be in control.'

So, too, even if death was an occupational hazard in his business, it was a factor which Judd had learned to be pragmatic about. 'The fact of the matter is that we are all mortal and we are all going to go. If I conceptually have to deal with that at a younger age, it's a bonus, it enhances the sweetness of the moments we have together,' she said, prior to clarifying her comments. 'This might defy credibility to

SNAPSHOTS OF AN INVISIBLE MAN

a lot of people, but racing is really safe. If you look at the statistics, you have got a greater chance of dying on the freeway or in a plane. Anyway, what can I do? At the end of the day, the universe unfolds the way that it wants to unfold.' And besides, there were other worlds to conquer.

Our next tryst with Dario occurs at the Rockingham circuit in Corby in England, where the Scottish driver was part of the ChampCar/CART business's attempt to preach to the unconverted in the United Kingdom, by highlighting how thrilling a spectacle they could stage for those motoring enthusiasts who were ready for something new. For much of the build-up to the 'Sure for Men' Rockingham 500, Franchitti served up a sterling imitation of a missionary, doing his best to instil knowledge in the natives, and he couldn't be faulted for the brio and banter he exchanged with a wide range of journalists on a whistle-stop tour of the country. I met him at the new offices of the *Scotsman* newspaper and he was, as usual, excellent company, both proclaiming the virtues of his vocation, ruminating on how much had changed since his early days in Edinburgh, and even allowing himself to be caught up in a manufactured battle between the 'Auld Enemies', when his car appeared at Rockingham with its livery modified to include a St Andrew's cross on its nosecone. 'It's my answer to Team St George,' he explained, in a reference to the first-ever all-England Champ Car team, with Darren Manning in the cockpit, and although there was a kitsch quality to some of the pre-race theatricals, they were no worse than one encounters whenever an American sport strives to 'break' Britain.

To be honest, this always seemed a hard sell to those of us who had listened to F1 supporters dish out disapproving opinions of the US-based series, but as he warmed up for the inaugural event, Franchitti spoke passionately about his affection for his roots and how he still made a point of returning home as often as his schedule would permit. 'On a nice summer's day, there is nowhere else like Scotland. I certainly don't ever want to come back here with an American accent or a mid-Atlantic drawl. Please shoot me first!' he told reporters, whilst Manning also indulged in talking up this so-called Battle of Britain. 'It is something we should be proud of, because English companies and British industry lead the world in motor racing,' said the youngster, in a speech which could have been cribbed – or 50 per cent of it at any rate – from Sir Jackie Stewart. 'I am a keen England football and cricket supporter and I wear my shirt with pride. It was very special to put on the Team St George overalls for the first time recently and I am really looking forward to Saturday afternoon and seeing all the England flags in the grandstands.'

This approach might have worked in a boxing context. But on the motoring circuit, Franchitti was in a different league to Manning and displayed his pedigree in front of a sizeable crowd with a convincing victory, amidst all the accoutrements of tartanry, bagpipes and kilts, and with several members of his family in attendance. He was piped to his car, and subsequently squeezed the life out of his rivals with an imperious display – despite suffering some initial problems which briefly threatened to derail him. None the less, the race was short on the thrills which had been promised in advance. Dario, deploying the tactical acumen which was one of his trademarks, was running near to the front for the majority of the event and profited on a late pit stop to secure the lead from Kenny Brack, as the prelude to fending off a belated challenge from Christian da Matta, eventually winning with an advantage of less than one second. At the finish, the bagpipes reverberated around the circuit anew, and one was reminded of Sir Thomas Beecham's response to a young mother who was seeking advice from the flamboyant conductor on what instrument she should encourage her child to learn, so as to avoid the traumas of having to endure excruciating practice sessions with the sawing of violins or discord of pianos. 'That is easy, madam, I would recommend the bagpipes,' boomed Beecham. 'They sound exactly the same when you can play them as when you can't.'

At the post-race press conference, da Matta and Patrick Carpentier, who had secured the second and third spots on the podium, began their chat without the victor, as another publicity stunt creaked into motion. As the Frenchman was in the midst of explaining his afternoon's work – 'I saw the leaders had traffic ahead, so there was something going on' – Dario suddenly entered the interview room with a piper marching in front of him playing 'Scotland the Brave', and, for a few ticks, nobody could quite believe what they were witnessing. However, once the shock had subsided, the moderator put this question to him: 'Dario, talk about this win. This must be a roller-coaster of emotions for you. You mum is here with you for the second time. You had some struggles early in the race, but you came back and, ultimately, the pits won it for you late in the race?'

It was a tortuous inquiry, worthy of Garth Crooks on an off day, but Dario was in ebullient mood. 'My mum, my grandmothers, my great aunt, they were all here and it was an interesting day. I knew we had a great car. In qualifying yesterday, I made a pretty bad job of it and we were still able to qualify reasonably near the front. At the start, it was very difficult to get around anybody, but luckily, Paul Tracy stayed away from me this time, so I was pretty grateful for that. [Laughter]. From that point, everything went fine. I came in for the first stop in order. But, trying to leave, I was on the limiter trying to slip the clutch and it just stalled. I thought initially that it was a traction control problem, so

I switched that off, but the same thing happened. Obviously, it was the clutch, so that put us to the back. But my team manager came up with a new strategy to get us out of sequence, and get us into some clean air. Everybody else came into the pits, so I got some pretty decent laps and I had a clear track. I could run pretty quickly, rather than the pace being dictated by the cars in front of me. We were hoping there was going to be a yellow when we wanted to come in, and that way, we could put a lap on the field. There wasn't a yellow, so we came out fourth, and that was certainly an improvement.

'Then we had a problem with one of the tyres. I thought it was a wheel bearing, initially. It was a vibration that was getting worse and worse. I came to the point that I couldn't pretty much see where I was going. So we had to make another pit stop. No problems. After that, it came down to the last pit stop. I've really been giving my guys a hard time this year about the pit stops, but if they ever needed to do one [well], that was a peach, it was right there. It was perfect. We came out in the lead and, after that, I could really stretch my legs and get going, because it cleared up pretty much the whole race, pretty much the last 30 laps. It's just terrific to win here, in my first oval race at home.'

This was articulate, and it was an accurate summation of what had happened at Rockingham, but the event also lacked a certain je ne sais quoi. Or, to be more blunt, it demonstrated that Champ Car was long on technical issues and Machiavellian tactics, but shorter on the visceral, nerve-shredding spontaneous action which had featured in so many of Dario's IndyCar assignments. Quite simply, it was akin to watching and listening to the now-defunct Scottish Claymores on their abortive mission to sell American Football to a new audience north of the Border. There was no doubting the sincerity or commitment of those involved in the enterprise, but what looked, sounded and felt right in a Stateside environment suddenly flopped when transported to a colder country where the notion of stiff upper lips and polite applause too often held sway over getting really excited.

In these terms, one of the less unexpected announcements was released at the end of the season, when Rockingham was removed from the 2003 schedules, after track officials conceded that hosting another Champ Car event would not be viable, due to the current economic climate. But if that was disappointing, it was also predictable and there was hardly a mass demonstration of fans ready to protest at the decision. If truth be told, the expensive exodus to Britain had merely exposed the limitations of speeding around ovals for a couple of hours and no amount of PR flim-flam could disguise that reality.

Franchitti, meanwhile, was about to enter the worst period of his professional career, his fourth-place position in the 2002 championship turning out to be the prelude to a sustained spell where it seemed that everything he touched turned to dross. There was little indication of the pain in store when he moved with the Andretti Green team to the Indy Racing League in 2003 – indeed, the switch brought a spark of excitement back into the picture after the sterility of the Champ Car chapters – but sometimes the most innocuous of incidents can snowball into a genuine crisis. And so it proved, when Franchitti sustained injuries in a motorbike accident, on a short trip back to West Lothian, in April, prior to linking up with his AGR colleagues in Japan. At first, the diagnosis did not sound overly serious – Dario's injury apparently consisted of a slight fracture of the L1 vertebra – but the situation quickly spiralled into a different proposition altogether. 'The bike [an MV Augusta motorcycle] had a mechanical problem,' explained Franchitti.

'I tried to slow down, but, of course, that was a bit difficult under the circumstances and I wound up crashing
through a hedge and landing on my back.' He was taken
by ambulance to St John's Hospital in Livingston, for prelim-
inary treatment and X-rays, and spent one night in the
Scottish New Town – only five miles away from his birth-
place in Bathgate. An MRI scan was subsequently conducted
at Ross Hall Hospital in Glasgow, which seemed to reveal
what the surgeon described as 'an anterior stable compres-
sion fracture of the L1 vertebra', with 'no posterior injury
or canal compromise'. Gobbledygook to the layman, but a
relief to the man in question.

Certainly, during the next few days, following his misfortune, neither Franchitti nor Michael Andretti had any sense
of the gravity of the problem. 'This is the first time in 19
years of racing that I have missed an event due to injury
and I am terribly disappointed to miss the Twin Ring race
in Motegi,' said Franchitti, who initially envisaged that he
might be out of action for a few weeks. 'It is a very important race for Honda, of course, and I am sorry that I won't
be able to be there with my team to get our first win at
Twin Ring Motegi. But I will have to be satisfied with rooting
for my team-mates at Andretti Green Racing – Dan
[Wheldon], Tony [Kanaan] and Michael [Andretti] – to get
the job done, which I know they are fully capable of doing.'
The words conveyed only a mild impatience and Andretti
was equally pragmatic as he contemplated a return to action
for Dario at the Indy 500. 'First and foremost, I am glad
Dario is okay. We need him 100 per cent healthy for the
rest of the season, because he is a vital part of this team.'

Yet, regardless of their hopes, matters were worse than
had originally been surmised. Franchitti had hoped to make
a speedy return to the United States, but instead, he received
treatment for three weeks in Scotland and even then, the

Family affair: Dario Franchitti has been indebted throughout his career to the support of his parents, George and Marina. Here he is in the early days of his career with another prize in Formula Vauxhall.
The Scotsman

Chicken run: Dario struggled to secure sponsorship as a teenager, but here he is benefitting from the backing of West Lothian-based firm, Marshall's Chunky Chickens. *The Scotsman*

Generations collide: Dario Franchitti and his compatriot, Allan McNish (far right), meet up with 11 year-old Lewis Hamilton – now a star of Formula One – at the 1996 Autosport International show in Birmingham. *LAT Photographic*

ter the Speedwagon: After arriving in the United States, a fresh-faced Franchitti propelled himself into spotlight by signing for Team Kool Green in 1998. *Zoran Milich, Getty Images Sport*

Best of enemies: As they battled for the 1999 IndyCar title, Franchitti and Colombia's Juan Pablo Montoya managed to enjoy a scooter ride together in Vancouver. *Kim Stallknecht, Getty Images*

Scaling the peaks: Motor sport has taken Dario Franchitti all round the globe and here he is competing against a dramatic backdrop in Monterrey, Mexico. *Robert Laberge, Getty Images Sport*

Opposite. Saltire in tyres: Dario has always been proud of his Scottish heritage and modified his helmet accordingly during the 2006 Indy 500 race in Indianapolis. *Gavin Lawrence, Getty Images Sport*

Local hero: When the CART series came to the British circuit of Rockingham in 2001, Dario sped to victory and raised the Scottish flag in front of his family. *Robert Laberge, Getty Images Sport*

Marathon men: Bryan Herta, Tony Kanaan and Dario Franchitti celebrate on the podium after winning the Mobil Twelve Hours of Sebring race in Florida in 2007. *Darrell Ingham, Getty Images Sport*

ate with destiny: Dario leads the field at the Indy 500 as the rain starts to fall on what was one of the ost fluctuating afternoons in the classic race's history. *LAT Photographic*

Arise gladiators: Dario stands ready on the front row of the grid at the 2007 Indy 500 event, a race whose thrilling outcome was to change his life forever. *Stan Honda, Getty Images*

Fame at last: As he sits in his AGR vehicle, next to the fabled Borg Warner trophy, Dario ponders the enormity of his magnificent triumph in the 2007 Indy 500. *Darrell Ingham, Getty Images Sport*

Leader of the pack: Having established himself as the man to beat, Franchitti discusses tactics during practice for the IRL Suntrust Indy Challenge in Richmond, Virginia. *Jamie Squire, Getty Images Sport*

Ahead of the game: Franchitti dominated much of the 2007 IRL championship and here he sits at the front in the Firestone Indy 400 in Brooklyn. *Jonathan Ferrey, Getty Images Sport*

Life in the spotlight: Dario and his wife, Ashley Judd, light up another red carpet while attending the ESPY awards at the Kodak Theatre in Hollywood in 2007. *Kevin Mazur, Getty Images*

Tactical battles: As Dario fought for the IRL title with New Zealand's Scott Dixon, he made a crucial pit stop in the season's thrilling denouement in Illinois. *Jamie Squire, Getty Images Sport*

The last hurrah: Dario and his colleagues within the AGR team celebrate his IRL championship success. But, within a few days, he announced he was moving to NASCAR. *Darrell Ingham, Getty Images Sport*

Eyes on the prize: After so many years of frustration, a beaming Franchitti holds the IRL championship trophy aloft, following his last-gasp victory over Dixon. *Darrell Ingham, Getty Images Sport*

The sorcerer's apprentice: Sir Jackie Stewart holds court with his fellow Scot, Franchitti, at the 2007 Autosport Awards at the Grosvenor House Hotel in London. *LAT Photographic*

The risk business: Mike Wallace spins out of control in front of Dario Franchitti in the NASCAR Busch Series in October 2007 in Memphis, Tennessee. *Kevin C. Cox, Getty Images Sport*

Perfect harmony: Dario has a rare moment to savour in 2008, after winning the 24 Hours of Daytona with his team mates, Memo Rojas, Scott Pruett and Juan Montoya. *LAT Photographic*

Battling for credibility: Dario knew he could expect no favours on his move to NASCAR and here he vies for supremacy in his No 42 Target Dodge in Arizona. *Jason Smith, Getty Images Sport*

Trouble in store: Scott Riggs collides with Franchitti at the Las Vegas Motor Speedway as the Scott's induction to NASCAR gradually turns into a long season in hell. *Jason Smith, Getty Images Sport*

problem was nowhere near being properly rectified. 'I was out of action for a couple of months, but eventually decided to compete at the Pikes Peak International Raceway and I finished fourth, which was pretty good, considering that I was in agony, and the pain got worse as the race went on,' Franchitti told me. 'My back hadn't healed at all. Not a bit of it. In fact, all that hanging around merely confirmed that surgery was required, which basically meant that a lot of what I was told by the doctors in Scotland was, well, rubbish.

'Finally, I went to the Methodist Hospital in Indianapolis, and was told that I needed an operation if I was to carry on racing. There were no ifs or buts about it. And, to be honest, there wasn't any debate either, not when you are as passionate about cars and racing as I have been since I was a wee boy.

'I was fortunate because I was in the hands of a renowned orthopaedic surgeon, Dr Terry Trammell, and his partner, Dr Larry Stevens, and they performed keyhole back surgery with a minimum of pain, and to such good effect that I was able to leave with Ashley and the rest of my family less than a week later. I had to wear a specially fitted carbon-fibre brace for a while and that was uncomfortable, but it was nothing compared to the alternative scenario. The medics told me they expected me to make a full recovery, and they were right. But it does show the thin dividing line which separates the best and the worst things in motor-sport.'

Franchitti added: 'It has been a difficult period, because I missed so many events in 2003 and I know that I have a lot of catching up to do and points to prove after the disappointments of the last year or so.'

By now, Dario had passed 30 and must have wondered whether he was ever destined to realise his true potential. Yet, if he imagined there would be any rapid respite, following his return to competitive action, he was soon to discover otherwise, regardless of his bullish attitude in the build-up to the IRL campaign in 2004. 'The early tests have been encouraging and we have been setting the pace, so if it boils down to two Britons scrapping for the title [himself and Wheldon], I would hope that we could raise the profile of the IRL back home. I know that F1 commands the lion's share of the attention in Europe and obviously I keep tabs on how the likes of David Coulthard and Juan Pablo [Montoya] are doing, but I really believe the IRL has the edge in terms of competitiveness.'

But, in truth, though he had fitted comfortably back into the AGR ranks, the tags of 'Invisible Man' and 'Mr Reliable' were starting to grate. Nobody could question his consistency in 2004, but, by the same token, his results were never sufficient for him to mount a credible bid and the optimists were reduced to clutching at a few positives which only amounted to underlying frustration. On the plus side, Dario enjoyed victories at Milwaukee and Pikes Peak, recorded eight top-ten finishes and qualified third in the Indy 500 – one of the prizes he cherished capturing the most – only to suffer problems in the race itself and end up in 14th position, which was a microcosm of the whole campaign. But there was a tangible sense of under-achievement as he was reduced to sixth in the IRL standings and 2005 brought a similar scenario, where the moments to savour were outnumbered by the weekends to forget. Once more, he prepared assiduously for the annual charge at the Brickyard and privately hoped that, on the 40th anniversary of his hero Jim Clark's success in the fabled Indianapolis race, he could deliver another Scottish success, particularly in the knowledge that Jackie Stewart was there to watch. The bond which had developed between these fellows from different generations was genuine: they cared for one another, and, given the frequent outbursts of macho posturing which occurred in the motoring world, there was something heart-warming about the manner in which Jackie and Dario were still thinking about Jimmy Clark, 37 years after the latter's death, and still striving to commemorate his life and legacy.

In short, the Indy 500 was the Holy Grail for these characters, an event whose fluctuations, nuances and diverse flows epitomised their pride in what they were doing. Every trip to the hallowed Brickyard offered another chance to gain a place in posterity, another opportunity to insert your name in the chronicles forever and Dario, who had initially struggled to grasp the enormity of the Indy 500, had steadily grown more and more transfixed with the notion of nailing the race and paying homage to Clark. Yet although Franchitti started from sixth place, and posted an impressive performance for much of the afternoon, a drastic loss of momentum, caused by his having to avoid another vehicle late in the proceedings, sent him back into the pack and consigned him to sixth, which was doubly exasperating because he knew it could and should have been better than that. 'I'm disappointed. The car was looking quite good before the last restart, when [France's Sebastien] Bourdais drove me into the wall. I am not quite sure what he was doing, but I guess that he paid the price in the end,' said Franchitti, with an air of resignation, which in the circumstances, might have been interpreted as silent fury. 'We didn't have enough right at the end. Some guys took track position and we got caught in the turbulence. We couldn't make our way through it, but Dan [Wheldon] could and the best of luck to him. He did a very good job out there and he deserved his Indy 500 victory.'

Once more, there was a feeling of deflation and a sense of being so near and yet so far. Again, as in the previous season, the lows exceeded the highs, with the latter basically restricted to a triumph on his home circuit at Nashville and an emotionally charged success in the denouement at Fontana, where his buddy, Moore, had perished, all those years before. There remained a suspicion that Franchitti had not lost, but merely mislaid, his mojo, but the statistics didn't lie – the sceptics were already sniping that he was a spent force and he was having to ask himself one or two major questions along the lines of: 'Do I want to do this anymore?' and 'Do I *need* to do this anymore?'

Yet, even as he reflected on these issues, his reaction to winning his 15th open-wheel race in Fontana demonstrated that the man's hunger was still undimmed. The event had been staged amid saturnine conditions and the outcome boiled down to the final few laps after the fourth and last caution period ended on lap 192. 'I could see Tony's car coming, but it was difficult to see as he was coming so quickly, but we were working together and we were starting to pull away from the other guys,' recalls Franchitti. 'It was a good team effort – we were all pulling for one another and you can help people around this circuit. It was a bitter-sweet win, because I lost a good friend here, and it was a tough day. We had a reasonably quick car, but we were very, very loose this morning in the warm-up, so we did some changes to that and it slowed us down. We just struggled with understeer a bit, but my crew did a fantastic job and we didn't make any mistakes out there when it mattered. You would think that somewhere as big and wide open as Fontana would be all about horsepower, but it is really a combination of the two. You have to get the car handling right here and the Andretti Green guys did a great job in that respect.'

From the outside, 2005 didn't appear that bad a year for Franchitti. He ended up fourth in the IRL championship, which meant that, at various stages, he had finished second, third, fourth and sixth in the standings during his career and, as usual, his commitment could not be doubted, while he amassed eight top-five and 13 top-ten results. But he wasn't quite the exuberant, bubbly presence of old and it was obvious that the accusations of being a 'nearly man' were embedding themselves in his brain, quite apart from his depression at missing out on the Indy 500 for reasons outwith his control.

'Jackie [Stewart], my old boss, came out for the race and it was looking good for a while, but it didn't pan out and I wasn't happy. I wasn't sure how much more I wanted to do, I wasn't that crazy about racing on ovals and the spark was kind of gone' said Dario, in explaining why he decided to sit down and discuss his future with the AGR team owners, Michael Andretti, Kim Green and Kevin Savoree. 'I was feeling good about the win [in Fontana], but I wasn't sure about some other things, so I decided to come back and see what would happen. But then, with the fairly average year that we had [in 2006], my motivation came back stronger than ever. I felt it again.' Which was just as well.

If nothing else, Franchitti's determination in the face of adversity meant that he was hell-bent on not being perceived as a quitter. He had survived crashes unscathed, emerged from an abundance of problems with his good nature and his confidence intact, and even as 2006 developed into a long summer in hell, he was desperate to do the right thing, not just for Ashley, who had difficulties of her own, but for the large number of employers and team-mates who had offered him loyalty since his initial foray into the American scene, when he had required guidance and camaraderie and found them both at Hogan Racing and since he had teamed up with the likes of Barry Green and Michael Andretti. On the track, his fortunes ebbed, and there were no victories and only a second at Sonoma and a third at Richmond to compensate for a series of disappointments as he plummeted down the championship rankings with a swiftness which made it more commendable that people such as Andretti kept the faith.

Away from the track, meanwhile, Ashley revealed, in the course of an interview with *Glamour* magazine, that she had spent 47 days in a Texas treatment facility for depression and a range of other emotional problems. She had entered the Shades of Hope Treatment Center in Buffalo Gap in February for 'co-dependence in my relationships; depression; blaming; raging; numbing, denying and minimising my feelings', and admitted that she had been in so much pain that she urgently required help, but had not taken the next step until making a visit to her sister, Wynonna, who was suffering from food addictions. Ashley explained: 'When [the counsellors] approached me about treatment, they said: "No-one ever does an intervention on people like you. You look too good; you are too smart and together. But you [and Wynonna] come from the same family, so you come from the same wound."' She added that, due to her chaotic childhood, when she attended 13 different schools in 12 years and lived alternatively with her mother, grandmother and father, she had become a 'hypervigilant' child, striving for impossible aims in life. 'A wonderful pastor once told me: "Perfectionism is the highest order of self-abuse." So, now I try to remind myself that if I engage in perfectionism, I am abusing myself. Period. It is so simple really. I was unhappy and now I am happy. Now, even when I am having a rough day, it's better than my best day before treatment.'

One can only speculate as to how Dario, born and bred into a rock-solid family unit, coped with these revelations, let alone how he had striven to prepare for the 2006 season while Ashley was in the Shades of Hope Center. But the fact that he had endured his worst campaign since arriving in the United States, almost a decade earlier, probably said enough without us intruding any further into private matters. For years now, one of the banes of covering sport has been the cynicism and even ridicule with which such issues as mental health are discussed – if they are discussed at all – and although there may be some people who feel uncomfortable with the language which Ashley employed to explain her experience at the Center, only a misanthrope would have dismissed her troubles. The important thing was that their marriage was stronger than ever by the end of what had been a troubled year for the couple: if they could survive these problems and stay intact, who knew how glorious life would be together in 2007?

7

THE SWEET TASTE

Dario Franchitti has always possessed a keen interest in the history of motor sport, and the personalities of the men who risked their lives in pursuit of glory long before the likes of Sir Jackie Stewart had successfully lobbied for greater safety around the globe's pits, paddocks, ovals and circuits. As a student of the business, and a connoisseur of the speed game, Franchitti was as well equipped as anybody to explain the enduring mystique and allure of the Indy 500, one of those events, like the Monaco Grand Prix and Le Mans, which, as he once remarked to me, should be on every driver's to-do list.

By the time Dario arrived at the Indianapolis Motor Speedway in May, 2007, he recognised that there might not be too many other opportunities to take the checkered flag at the home of the Brickyard and Victory Lane, but he continued to revel in the brilliance which his hero, Jim Clark, had brought to the annual extravaganza. If there had been any justice, Clark, relentlessly imperious and effortlessly indomitable at the wheel, should have won the Indy 500 on at least three occasions. In 1963, his rear-engined Lotus was the best car in the field, only for Clark's aspirations to be stymied when officials turned a blind eye to an oil leak on the leading Watson roadster of the flamboyant American competitor, Parnelli Jones, and while the Scot was badly hampered by the lubricant when in hot pursuit of his rival, the home racer held on. Undeterred, Clark was back the following spring, and led the proceedings until suffering mechanical failure. And then, most controversially of all, in 1966, England's Graham Hill was adjudged the champion, even though Clark was convinced that the presiding officials had missed one of his laps, allowing the raffish Hill to swap his normal tipple for some milk – it was the traditional sustenance for the winners, as a gift from the local dairy-farming community, which has become one of the myriad customs etched in Indy 500 folklore.

However, as Franchitti knew, Clark has been utterly majestic in sweeping to his goal in 1965, displaying a combination of derring-do and clinical precision, which evoked awe amongst all those who witnessed his pyrotechnics. The Borderer, as modest and unassuming out of the car as he was a volcanic presence within the cockpit, might have perished in Germany in 1968, but his memory lingered on undiminished. Franchitti had steeled himself to celebrate the 40th anniversary of that stunning performance with a repeat showing in 2005, and was buoyed by the news his old mentor, Stewart, was there to cheer him on. But sadly, the script didn't go according to plan. On the plus side, a Briton triumphed – in the guise of England's Dan Wheldon – but there was only misery and frustration for Franchitti, who clattered out of contention and said later: 'I'm pissed.' Not through alcohol, but from the sheer anti-climax of being reacquainted with failure.

In these circumstances, Dario could surely have been forgiven for being tetchy, cantankerous even, in the build-up to the battle on Sunday, May 27. At the age of 34, he had slipped into the role of his team's faithful retainer, with the majority of the headlines devoted to his Andretti Green racing colleagues, whether it was Danica Patrick, Tony Kanaan, or focused around the idiosyncratic temperaments of the Andretti clan. By comparison, Franchitti was the solid citizen, the chap who preferred anonymity to the spotlight, or, as he was described rather insultingly in several publications, 'Mr Judd'.

Yet, befitting his dry-as-Nevada wit and his appreciation of the potency of letting actions speak louder than words, he carried out his media requests with the usual understated aplomb. Elsewhere, it appeared that whole of America had touched down in the city. Paul Newman was present, so too Ray Liotta and Sylvester Stallone. There were assorted cast members from the television series *Desperate Housewives*, *Grey's Anatomy*, *Heroes* and *The Riches*, whilst a raft of the NFL and MLB's bankable assets indicated that they would grace the event with one eye on the paparazzi and the other in search of undercover drug testers. Ashley Judd was also there, of course. But there again, as the sport's cognoscenti had observed, there were few weekends when she didn't stand by her man.

In essence, it was merely another photo opportunity for the United States' bright young things, which possibly explained why Franchitti almost yawned in discussing matters off the track. 'Perhaps it sounds strange, but I don't notice the cameras any more. Ashley does, but I have learned to blend into the background, and that suits me, because there are plenty of things to be concentrating on here, without getting caught up in the hype,' he told me, 72 hours before the Indy crusade. 'To be honest, I love this race and I marvel at everything which surrounds it. Every spring, when it looms into view, and we climb onto the plane, I am like a little kid again. You are here in Indianapolis for three weeks before the race and most of your waking hours are occupied in preparing for one of the greatest days in the motoring calendar. I mean, you are following in the footsteps of legends. Jim Clark, Graham Hill, Emerson Fittipaldi, Al Unser, A J Foyt . . . these guys' names will never be forgotten and the thought of joining them on the winners' roster sends chills up my spine.'

By this stage of the conversation, Franchitti had drifted into the language of a dewy-eyed dreamer, but that merely accentuated his burning desire to secure this coveted prize, after so many previous disappointments. Having spent a decade in the United States, his career had been frustratingly stop-start, his ambitions intermittently blighted by injury, mechanical glitches, the unsought intervention of bad weather, or Dame Misfortune, and his critics might have been able to argue that his potential had gradually dissipated. Yet, such a perfunctory analysis so patently ignored his welter of achievements in both Indy Cars and Champ Cars, let alone the wealth he had amassed, that anybody querying Franchitti's track record was in danger of sounding akin to the hotel porter who once asked George Best – champagne, Miss World et al – where it all went wrong.

Nor was there any denying his commitment as the hours ticked down to the Indy 500. 'I accept there have been problems in the last couple of seasons – the car wasn't fast enough last year, end of story – but I have done alright so far in this IRL campaign [he lay fourth in the standings] and it is definitely time I improved my record at the Indy 500, because I know the circuit, I know my capabilities and those of my team-mates, and I have never been interested in looking for excuses. Back in 2005, I led the race for a few laps and I was starting to think to myself: "Hey, wouldn't it be fantastic to have another Scottish success story on the 40th anniversary of Jim Clark's victory here?" Big mistake! Soon afterwards,

I suffered a steering problem, and had to do a pit stop, then I crashed out and that was the dream extinguished for another 12 months. That taught me, as if I wasn't already aware of it, that you should never assume anything in this game.

'But listen [when he cranks up his discourse, Franchitti can rapidly become as animated as Homer Simpson], I have a model of the car which Jim drove when he won here and I am 100 per cent convinced that I can follow in his footsteps. By my reckoning, there are ten of us, maybe 11, who can win this weekend and I am starting on the front row, behind [the Brazilian duo] Helio Castroneves and Tony Kanaan, so I am in the right position to mount a challenge and bring home the big prize for Andretti Green Racing.

'Basically, I am fascinated by what makes things tick and that includes both engines and human beings. Every race is different and you have to devise the right strategy, think on your feet, and be ready to be flexible if the circumstances demand it. The Indy 500, for example, is not that physical a test, but mentally, it is very, very hard and you are shot to pieces by the finish, because it is a game of centimetres and millimetres, of tight margins between success and failure, and when you look at the weather forecast for the next few days, it could be wet and that means there could be another major factor to worry about.'

The words were remarkably prescient, but there again, Franchitti had experienced sufficient slings and arrows during his career to be conscious of the fickle nature of fast-lane existence. What shone through was his fascination and near-obsession with the minutiae of the Indy 500, and as he talked, it was easy to comprehend why so many Americans regard this event as the greatest spectacle in motor racing. For starters, unlike the sleek, shiny but frequently tedious environs of Formula One, the race places more emphasis on drivers than manufacturers, meaning that the best of the bunch will usually prevail. Secondly, there are no short cuts to success, ensuring that precious few competitors negotiate the Indianapolis Motor Speedway, originally built on 328 acres of farmland, north-west of Indiana's capital city in 1909, at their first or second attempt. Instead, this is a challenge which requires the sort of local knowledge that is only amassed through experience, even if the total purse – in excess of $10m – guarantees there is never any shortage of participants willing to follow the lead of somebody such as Franchitti's rival, Scott Dixon, who prepared for his Indy tour of duty by training at an altitude of 9,000 feet to make his body more efficient at absorbing oxygen.

The buzz of expectation which permeated the Brickyard on that Sabbath afternoon reflected the open nature of the contest. Nor, once it commenced, with a script featuring the vagaries of the climate, a mass of fluctuations resulting from a diversity of tactics and a bewildering array of scheduled or enforced pit stops, was there anything less than all-encompassing drama of the kind which explains why movies about sport rarely transcend cliché and soap. During the first 30 laps, the pole-sitters, Castroneves and Kanaan were involved in half-a-dozen lead changes, and Franchitti seemed to be struggling with technical issues, necessitating some swift remedial treatment. 'We went out there today and had a huge push in the car. We had to work very hard to get rid of that. There was a big understeer, but I was very impressed with the job the engineers did. This was about split-second decisions, but they made the right choices. They were talking to me, in constant communication with me, and I was making adjustments in the car all the time. But it was going in the right direction, which was really helpful, because coming back through the pack at that point, I thought

I was going to have to pick off one car at a time, and see where we ended up, which is never an easy job anywhere. We just had to keep our minds on the job and focus on all the things that we could control.'

In front of him, the race was a maelstrom of incident, with five competitors – Roberto Moreno, John Herb, Milka Duno, John Andretti and Phil Giebler – crashing out of contention. Moreno's accident, which happened when he entered a turn too high, and struck a wall, led to a caution period, while the wreck was removed. As the pressure intensified, Castroneves suffered serious pit problems when his crew struggled to refuel his vehicle, which consigned him to the rear of the field. Yet, if one Brazilian was in the wars, his compatriot, Kanaan, was enjoying a superb outing in his AGR car, and seemed poised for victory when he took the lead by passing his team-mate, Andretti, after 108 laps, even as the clouds darkened over the packed circuit. By this juncture, Franchitti had climbed to fifth place, and lay within striking distance of the leaders, but when the heavens opened at 3.02pm, as the meteorologists had correctly predicted, just less than two hours after the start, the door looked to have been slammed shut on his hopes. The bad weather brought an immediate halt to the proceedings, and while Kanaan couldn't afford to relax, he knew that if there was no further action, the Indy 500 title was in the bag. As for the pursuing pack, they simply had to ignore negative thoughts and wait, wait, wait, even if the TV satellite forecast shots offered naught for their comfort.

'We talked about strategy, how we would behave, how we would try and ensure that an AGR car finished in the winning position. We had some fun as well, cracked a couple of jokes, just tried to ease the tension a bit, and sat in engineering with our feet up,' said Franchitti. 'We also had a little bit of pasta. The guys at hospitality made us a nice bowl of it and that was very tasty. We couldn't afford to sweat over what might or might not happen and it was probably worse for Tony, because he was in the No 1 spot.

'In fact, when the red flag came out, it was one of those bittersweet moments for me. I'm seeing Tony leading the race and looking like he's going to win the thing. I'm thinking: "You know, I reckon my car is good enough to get the job done here", but, on the other side of the coin, my best friend is leading the race and my two other team-mates [Marco Andretti and Danica Patrick] are in second and third places. Yet the selfish part of me was also thinking: "I hope we can go back out racing", because I really fancied my chances. But that happens in these situations: there are all sorts of conflicting emotions passing through your mind and that would have been the same for everybody else.'

As the loitering continued, Franchitti reflected on several different issues. He wondered whether his father, George, had used up the family's ration of luck for the week by achieving a hole-in-one – his first ace – at the Brickyard Crossing golf course on the previous Wednesday. He also mused on the past disappointments in Indianapolis and asked himself whether the gremlins were forever destined to plague him on these grand occasions. But, considering the chaos which had engulfed the arena, with 350,000 spectators unsure of whether their sport had concluded for the day, to a backdrop of frantic energy from mechanics, engineers and climate experts, the Scot was surprisingly calm in the midst of bedlam. He later told me that some of this was down to his own perspective on life: that, as long as he had done his best and could return to the bosom of his family, no mere sporting event was worth fretting over to the point of becoming a ticking timebomb of insanity. Of course, he was on edge and naturally, when the information eventually reached the drivers that the race would begin again at

6.01pm, his adrenaline was flowing. But he never surrendered his composure or his conviction that if history was in the making, he might as well be the man to force the issue when it mattered.

And yet, would any author dare to have penned such a climax? Franchitti was still in fifth place when he cut a tyre – the consequence of running over debris – as the racers headed towards a lap 114 restart, following the three-hour delay, and he was forced to pull into the pits, putting him onto a different schedule from his rivals. On another afternoon, it might have destroyed his chances, but, with gloomy clouds rolling round, over and on top of the Brickyard, a motoring joust had developed into a crap-shoot on wheels. 'I guess we ran over some carbon from the last accident and we had to pit. That wasn't our intention, but we had to do it for safety reasons and it worked in our favour which I am . . . pretty happy about. But it's an interesting thing to go through, this whole Indy 500 thing, because you have to put all your eggs in one basket and this only comes along once a year. It really hit me on lap 113, when we thought the race was finished. That was it, and we figured that our chance had vanished for another season, because you put so much into it, everybody in the team puts so much into it, and then it can be over in a flash. If you saw the way our team worked together, how hard the engineers worked back at the shop, along with the mechanics, to get these cars quick, and realised how much effort they had put in to make the difference between last year and this time, it made you really really proud to be a part of the whole process. We have five drivers and five sets of engineers, and it is bloody impressive when the whole lot comes together.'

In the Indy 500 build-up, there had been several references in the American newspapers to Franchitti and Dixon as 'the invisible men'. They eschewed trash talk, refused to indulge in hype, and were lacking the gender angle of Danica Patrick or the wunderkind on the blocks potential of the 20-year-old Marco Andretti. Yet there are instances where flying under the radar can have beneficial side effects and this was one of them. As Franchitti returned to the fray in Indianapolis, the other AGR drivers were knocking six or seven bells out of one another and nobody's eyes were on the Scot. Andretti grabbed the lead anew on lap 116, but Kanaan soon overtook him once more, and as the former crashed out and the latter had to go into the pits, Franchitti was suddenly presented with a massive opportunity, which opened up in front him, like a blinding light. He was at the helm, with the elements worsening, the blackness of the clouds hinting at impending rain. He held his nerve, maintained his sangfroid, and, oblivious to the ubiquitous Ashley whooping and hollering with delight as the denouement beckoned, he stuck to the routine, adhered to the principles which had brought him success in the IRL, and rode towards glory. Nobody was pretending, least of all Dario himself, that he didn't enjoy the rub of the green, amber and red. And he profited from two further caution periods, one which began on lap 157 when Jacques Lazier collided with a wall, causing Kanaan to swerve which saw him suffer a puncture, as the prelude to another on lap 163 when Andretti's car flipped over after making contact with Dan Wheldon's vehicle.

The concern now was whether Franchitti had enough fuel to carry him home, but he knew the weather was closing in with an inexorable haste. If the race had continued for much longer, he would have relinquished the lead, which had already changed hands no fewer than 24 times. But, in this instance, there was no disappointment; there were no tales of what might have been, or sickening reports from an ambulance crew elsewhere. Instead, there was a level of jubilation on his march into Victory Lane which extended beyond simple success and encompassed all manner of emotions: relief, pride, comfort and vindication, allied to a tangible reminder of the virtues of collectivism. Even as his colleagues sought him out, Ashley embraced her husband, and rational thought could whistle awhile.

'I knew TK [Tony Kanaan] was going to kiss me. I knew it. That was a given. I was really happy to see Marco and find out that he was okay. When I saw his accident, and saw the aftermath of it, I was on the radio, asking: "Is he okay? Is he okay?" So, just to see him there at the end was a massive relief. I think the disbelief started when the rain came on again, then it turned into a downpour, and I was thinking it was going to be difficult reaching the finish, because the car was aquaplaning, it was so wet out there. Then, eventually, I got to the finish line and it was just disbelief coming into the pits. I came in really slowly, first of all because I didn't want to crash the car on the in-lap, and also to acknowledge that the crowd had stayed on patiently throughout all the rain delay and got absolutely soaked, and they deserved to enjoy the moment as well as me.

'Towards the end, well, obviously the weather was causing me some anxiety. The one comment that sticks in my mind was [AGR technician] John Anderson saying on the radio: "The rain is eight blocks away." And I am like: "C'mon, let's go for it." When you get in that position, we knew we had to pit one more time, but we were pretty much sure that everybody else would also have to go into the pits, so it was going to come down to a serious dogfight. There are a lot of strong cars in the field, especially among my team mates, the Ganassi guys, the Penske guys . . . that's a lot of competition. But whatever happened, it was going to be hard in that dogfight and I was hoping for the rain.

'But now it is done, what else can I say! I'm in shock at this point. I am definitely in shock. It was exciting, and when I had to fight my way back through the pack, I managed to get through the traffic pretty quickly and get back into contention. Then, the strategy, our roll of the dice, proved to be the right one. We got in front, made a couple of good restarts, then the rain came. It's been a roller-coaster month and a roller-coaster day. But what a day! I mean, any one of the [AGR] cars could have won out there today, and it came down to, you know, there was some luck involved. But that is not to diminish what we achieved today. That's just a reflection of the brilliant job the team did – that they put five cars on the grid and all of them were capable of winning. But it all kind of made sense when I turned round and looked at the Indy 500 trophy. I saw some of the great names on it and I was awe-struck, I really was. It's a very humbling experience.'

The next few hours elapsed as if a higher presence was shooting a motorised version of 'Sleepless in Seattle', which featured a limitless array of images to delight romantics everywhere. At the crowning moment of triumph, impervious to the conditions, Ashley skipped merrily across the Brickyard's terrain, splashed into puddles with the carefree, go-hang attitude of a five-year-old child, waved deliriously to anybody who crossed her path, and flashed the broadest of smiles, without anybody requiring to cry 'Cut!' Even the sky, so morose and threatening in the earlier scenes, was illuminated by sunshine, in the midst of a springtime shower, and such was the air of shock and surprise in the air that nobody would have batted an eyelid if Dario's No 1 fan had started singing and dancing in the rain. As it was, she held her high heels in her hands, and lolloped barefoot down the pit road with a touch of the spontaneity and pizazz which the cynics claimed had deserted the Indy 500, as the prelude to leaping into the arms of the 'invisible man', who had suddenly dramatically emerged from the shadows.

'One by one,' she said, 'Dario picked the other drivers off, and he was fantastic. And this is *waaaay* overdue.'

The limelight can be an intimidating place, but not for those who have sweated and toiled to shatter perceptions and Dario could afford to luxuriate in his overnight transformation from unheralded professional to international superstar. For more than two hours at the Indianapolis Motor Speedway, he stood in front of the cameras, posing for pictures with every single crew member from his AGR team, satisfying the autograph demands of a hyper-ventilating bevy of sponsors and track officials, and trying to make sense of the enormity of his achievement. 'At times,' recalled Damian Dottore, an estimable Stateside journalist with the *Orange County Register*, whose coverage of the event attained the rare feat of avoiding mawkishness or Tinseltown fakery while vividly bringing the ceremonials to life. 'the line was stretched as long as a football field. Everyone in Indiana, or so it appeared, wanted to be in the company of the new Indy 500 winner. While they waited, Ashley chatted with them as she took her dog for a walk, and it was during one of those rare quiet moments in between the pandemonium, when Franchitti caught a glimpse of a few of the names on the Borg-Warner Trophy, and his emotions finally started to get the better of him.'

'I am not sure what this means just yet. I know it is huge. This is the biggest race we do and it is amazing and special,' said Franchitti, as he circled the circuit in the passenger seat of one of the track's white Chevrolet vans. 'It is amazing to think that this trophy . . . I . . . I am really going to be on it. It's a massive honour, and even now, it is difficult to take in. but it is slowly starting to sink in . . .'

Around the track environs, Franchitti's colleagues congratulated his success with a warmth and sincerity which reflected his popularity. There was a wonderful tribute from Kanaan, who had every right to feel disconsolate about the fashion in which fate had dashed his own ambitions, but the two men were like brothers as they walked away for a private conversation, with the Brazilian echoing the sentiments of the majority of the crowd. 'If it had to be somebody else rather than me, thank God it was Dario, because the man has been inspirational in the way he has recovered from setbacks and returned to action stronger than ever.' Even as Franchitti partook of the winner's traditional milk, two generations of Andrettis joined in the paeans. 'I am one lucky guy,' said Marco, unbowed by the terrifying crash from which he has strolled away unscathed. 'I was upside-down in the car, just praying to God. If I had gone through that and somebody from another team had won, I wouldn't be happy, to put it mildly. But I am just so proud of Dario and what he did out there. He kept plugging away and got his due reward.' For the team owner, Michael Andretti, the outcome of the race might have extended his family's jinx at the Brickyard, but he was effusive in his response. 'Dario deserves this. He has been such an important part of the organisation since Day 1 and he has been a big part in getting us to where we are today that everybody is delighted for him, and I reckon that opinion will be shared pretty much right across the whole of motor sport, because Dario is a helluva nice guy and this proves that good things really do happen to good people.'

Across the water, meanwhile, Sir Jackie Stewart was striving to make contact with his former prodigy, to proffer his own congratulations with his habitual Panglossian positivity. For the previous 40 years, having famously overcome scholastic problems caused by his own undiagnosed dyslexia, he had been an articulate, relentlessly sedulous roving ambassador for his country, whether nurturing Scotland's brightest motoring prospects through his 'Staircase of Talent'

or highlighting his belief that his nation's biggest export is
not whisky or shortbread, but rather human beings blessed
with ideas, innovation and leadership qualities, and Stewart,
as he told me with a trill in his voice, believed that Franchitti
had embodied all these traits even in his reaction to victory.

'I have just heard about Dario and it is an immensely
thrilling result, because he has gone over to the United States
and risen above misfortune, he has kept persevering, and
proving his worth, and now his name is in the archives
forever,' said Stewart, prior to embarking on one of his
fabled stream-of-consciousness declarations, which actually
cut to the chase in defining Dario's advance up the Stateside
ladder. 'I honestly believe that we Scots are a unique group
of people and that there is something distinctive about the
Scottish psyche, which stamps us out from every other
country. Maybe it is part of our inferiority complex that we
try harder to make our name in the world and I have never
forgotten that when I first travelled to England, I was
absolutely convinced the locals down there thought I was this
daft wee laddie with haggis growing out of my ears.

'Yet that simply made me more determined, more driven
and focused on proving that I could be every bit as good
as them, if not better than them, and I think we have a sense
that, because we hail from a small nation, we have to aim
higher to get noticed. You see it in business, and you look
at the philanthropy of somebody such as Sir Tom Hunter,
and there is the same generosity, breadth of vision, and desire
to improve things than was in the genes of Andrew Carnegie.
You see it in show business, where Sir Sean Connery is one
of the most recognisable figures on the planet, and yet he
still wants to change things by speaking out on issues which
concern him. [Such as the increasingly relevant subject of
whither Scottish independence]. And you see it in motor-
sport, where we have punched above our weight in terms

of producing world champions in Formula One, in rallying, and other categories, and I think it boils down to us wanting to be taken seriously and do things which will make other Scots proud of us. You have to stick to your principles, but when you are a young man going out into the world, such as Dario Franchitti, you have to show dedication, commitment, resilience, enthusiasm, gratitude, team spirit and a passionate belief in your own ability, and Dario has done all of those things from an early stage. It boils down to some central tenets of philosophy: never think you are bulletproof; never take anything for granted; never adopt the corporate strut; and, for heaven's sake, never ever start to believe that the world owes you a living.

'I always regarded Dario as a top-class talent, right from the outset. In the early 1990s, he was a leading driver for Paul Stewart Racing, the team I formed with my son, and when he went to America, I was certain he would become a force to be reckoned with there. He was out of racing for a while after injuring his back in a motorbike accident and some people thought that it might have destroyed his whole career. So it is tremendous for him to come back and win something like the Indy 500 after a lot of people wrote him off. He is well grounded, he has kept his head out of the clouds, and stuck by the values which he grew up absorbing, and that has meant he knows what is and isn't important in life. Dario has never lost his Scottishness or his accent, he is very straightforward, easy-going off the track, and he hasn't changed at all, despite all his fame and becoming a celebrity. The bottom line is he enjoys his life to the max and is one of the nicest men I know.'

As character references go, this can't be far from being a perfect testimonial. But, there again, Stewart had competed twice at the Brickyard and had learned to appreciate the trials and travails inherent in aspiring to collect one of motor-sport's grandest honours. What further impressed him about Franchitti was the man's fortitude in bouncing back from the litany of woes which befell him in 2006, where it would have been easy for a lesser individual to slip into depression as weeks of disappointment banked up like the planes over Heathrow Airport. Yet, although Dario didn't deny he had felt deflated at the lowest points of the sequence, and had actually considered whether the desire burned as strongly inside him as it had once done, he wasn't and had never been a quitter.

On the contrary, whether casting his gaze back to the strife he had encountered in 1999 or 2003, or reflecting on the interminable sequence of glitches which would have left less mild-mannered individuals foaming at the mouth throughout 2006, Franchitti could relax as the hours unfolded after his Brickyard heroics. Henceforth, whatever happened in his career, here was one tangible triumph which nobody could ever take away from him; his inscription along-side legends, conclusive evidence that his gifts had gained proper recognition, not in terms of dollars or newspaper column inches – although there were plenty of these as well – but with the rare alchemy of graft, grit, glamour and glitter of those who bestride their pursuits and achieve the highest accomplishments.

No wonder, therefore, that Franchitti changed in the wake of his Indy 500 win. The transformation was noted by those who knew him best. 'He looks like he is walking lighter, almost as if he is walking on air,' remarked Danica Patrick. 'It allows you to take stock and enjoy having the pressure off,' said the 2005 victor, Dan Wheldon, who added: 'People talk about the magnitude of this event, but what amazes me is that it relaxes us so much more. We have done something which will never be forgotten.' Sam Hornish Jnr – who was crowned champion at the Brickyard in 2006 – was even more emphatic. 'Once you have got that monkey off your back, it allows you to have more fun. I'm sure that a lot of the guys on the IRL circuit would say it has had that effect on me being able to open up and be a lot more approachable,' said Hornish, who had grown up in nearby northwest Iowa and been burdened, from an early age, with local observers tipping him for stardom. 'Once you have won here, there isn't anything like as much pressure on you, because nothing can take away the sweet taste which the Indy 500 gives you.'

The symbiosis between those who lift the title was amplified by the manner in which Franchitti sought out Hornish for a post-race breaking of the frost which had previously existed in the relationship between the two drivers. Dario, calm-as-you-please, suave in his media dealings and blessed with finely-hored PR skills, was ripe Camembert to his dour, deadpan American rival's chalk, and yet, when the pair met for an exhibition of glasnost in the middle of the night at a downtown Indianapolis nightclub called 6, it was as if they had morphed into the Chuckle Brothers. 'Sam and I got involved in some sort of misunderstandings from pretty much the first day I joined the IRL and I just thought to myself: "Hey, what the hell!" So, I sat down and talked with him, and we shared our experiences of life, on and off the race track, and we had such a good time together that the hours just melted away. We chatted about all different kinds of stuff and got to know the other's views and thoughts, and it was cool.' Hornish, for his part, described the couple's 45-minute conversation as 'stunning' and related how the interaction had bought the memories of his own success flooding back. 'If you would have told me a month ago that this would be happening, I would have said you were crazy, but it's amazing how you can break down barriers by sitting down and talking to somebody and that is exactly what materialised with Dario and myself,' said Hornish. 'I was trying to get out of there at, like, 3.30 or 4 in the morning, and he was still chewing the breeze and we were reminiscing over the whole history of the Indy 500 and what being winners of the event meant to us. I was like: "I know what you have in store for you tomorrow." But Dario was like: "No sweat, we can cross that bridge when we get to it." And we walked away with respect and admiration for the other. Which is pretty great, isn't it!'

The next few days turned into a giddy whirl of incessant promotional activities for both Franchitti and Judd, with the former's stamina and endurance tested to the limit. One solitary hour of sleep followed the victory party, but he manfully answered a crack-of-dawn wake-up call and embraced a punishing schedule of talk-show interviews, Q & A sessions and all manner of diverse inquiries from television networks, corporate press offices and petrolheads alike, with the smile and ready patter of somebody groomed for this attention by Jackie Stewart all those years ago. It wasn't, after all, as if he was being interrogated by Jeremy Paxman or John Humphrys, but rather patting back softly-softly queries from doting acolytes and motoring aficionados such as David Letterman, whose love affair with those who pervade the pit and paddock is the stuff of legend. In which circumstances, Franchitti relished the spotlight – and why not? His life story was a million miles more interesting than that of some of the bland automatons who inhabit Formula One (and other sports) and who have less expression on their faces than their backsides. Naturally, there were instances, as the circus progressed, where he felt that he had repeated himself to the stage where he was imprisoned within his own private 'Groundhog Day', but any grumbles were easily suppressed. When asked after his win if the increasing demands on his time – whether on *Letterman*, Sky Sports,

BBC Scotland, or fulfilling wackier assignments, such as a guest spot on ESPN's *Pardon the Interruption* – were proving a distraction, Judd interjected with the retort: 'Ask *me*!' as the precursor to her husband's reply. But, as Dario explained to me later in the year, he could scarcely quibble over the furore when all his prayers had been answered.

'I would definitely have liked some more time at home, hanging out with Ashley. But, as Scott Dixon put it so well: "You get paid for all the PR stuff. You drive the car because you want to." One of the nicest things about winning the 500, and there have been millions of them, was the fact that everybody who has won before came up and said: "Welcome to the club." That's cool, and it kind of sums up the atmosphere amongst the racers, because we all go out and work our hardest to beat one another, but we are friends once we have crossed the finish line. That's true, not only for the people in the cars, but also the hundreds of unsung heroes who work behind the scenes and do a fantastic job, without ever seeing their names in light. At Andretti Green Racing, the whole engineering staff have been magnificent this year, especially Allen McDonald and Dave Seiffert and John Anderson, and I wouldn't have won the Indy 500 without these guys spending countless hours improving things to the nth degree.

'That is another thing which strikes me about what has happened here in Indianapolis. Namely, that a group of us at AGR sat down in 2005 and talked about what might happen in the future. I wasn't sure. I was just being honest, but I wasn't sure how much longer I wanted to carry on. Then, when we had a fairly average season in 2006, my motivation came back stronger than ever, because I didn't want to leave on a downbeat note. Now, whatever happens, I don't see me quitting any time soon. You know, one of the things that really helps us to start fresh is having a 20-year-old team mate.

Seriously. TK and I are old married men now, but to see things through Marco's eyes is a breath of fresh air and it keeps us all young. I've had some fantastic team-mates in my life, some inspirational colleagues, but I don't think we will ever have this situation again.'

Back in Dario's homeland, his exploits hadn't gone unnoticed. Alex Salmond, the newly-anointed First Minister of the SNP minority administration in the Scottish Parliament, sent Franchitti a message of congratulations, adding that the characteristically Scottish weather may have enhanced his prospects. 'It was a tremendous performance and he clearly had the elements on his side as well,' observed Salmond. The Justice Minister, Kenny MacAskill, was equally laudatory, whilst making a valid point about the fashion in which Scotland seems to treat its non-footballing sports stars with a depressing fickleness. 'Scotland does not have a multitude of sporting stars to choose from and many of our national teams are currently in the doldrums. Yet Scots are keen to celebrate the success of sporting compatriots and this has been done throughout the years, and not just with successful football sides or Grand Slam-winning rugby teams,' opined MacAskill. 'Boxers such as Ken Buchanan and Jim Watt, swimmers like Bobby McGregor or David Wilkie, athletes like Allan Wells and Liz McColgan, darts world champion, Jocky Wilson, and the Olympic gold-medal-winning Olympic curling rink – all have seen the nation tune in, hoping for a Scottish victory, and taking these individuals to their collective hearts.

'Scotland would also follow the exploits and endeavours of Dario Franchitti with the same zeal, if only they were able to do so, and could read about him and watch him perform. Our media have to take some responsibility for reporting on him and fostering support for Scottish international success, at home and abroad. It's not simply that we want to back our compatriots and are desperate for them to shine at sport, whatever it might be. Dario is also an excellent role model. He is highly successful in a highly competitive environment. A clean-cut young man, he is highly presentable with little vanity and no bad habits. As we seek to tackle the serious problems of delinquency and anti-social behaviour, Scotland should be promoting him, not ignoring him. He is big in the Big Country. It's time that he was also big in his own country.'

It was a relevant message in a nation where the Old Firm command banner headlines at the height of summer and where absurd transfer non-stories and trivial tittle-tattle fill up the pages of even the so-called quality press. Yet, for Dario at least, there was nothing to be gained from whingeing over his anonymity in his homeland: a state of affairs which spared him from having to stave off unwelcome intrusions into his private life. And, besides, having triumphed at the Brickyard, there was an IRL title to chase.

8

A FIGHT FOR GREATER RECOGNITION

Motor-sport has a battalion of detractors, who argue that it shouldn't be regarded as a genuine test of human endeavour, because the driver in the best car usually carries off the main prize, thus ensuring that even somebody with Michael Schumacher's prodigious gifts would have struggled in Formula One had be been stuck in a Super Aguri vehicle. It's an argument not without merit, but the dramatic twists and turns which proliferated both in F1 and the Indy Racing League throughout 2007 offered a persuasive rejoinder to the cynics. After all, only a curmudgeon would have failed to derive at least slivers of delight from the exploits of Lewis Hamilton on his induction to the Grand Prix ranks, where the English wunderkind seemed destined to soar to championship glory before being deprived of the title, largely as a consequence of his own frailties, in the last two races of a season which encompassed every nuance and scintilla of visceral emotion from a pursuit sometimes perceived as being a procession of monochrome mediocrity.

Yet if that was a magical mystery tour of the world's

chicanes, the IRL campaign, in some respects, was even more unpredictable, not least because Dario Franchitti seemed to discover new means of generating publicity, increasing pulse rates, and keeping his friends and rivals alike in a state of perpetual disbelief as the summer advanced. There was the mastery of his early performances, through the cul-de-sac of imperial quality which constituted his victory in the Indy 500 at the Brickyard, and thereafter he embarked on a white-knuckle ride beyond anything found at Disney World, embracing thrilling racing, fractious internecine warfare, heart-stopping crashes and a climax to the story which would have been ridiculed as OTT by any smart Hollywood operator.

As the dust gradually settled around Indianapolis, the common opinion, amongst the IRL fraternity, seemed to be that Franchitti would sweep to the championship, carried along on a crescendo of momentum, generated by his exploits on the road to Victory Lane. It was a compelling conviction, if for no other reason than that Dario himself responded to the pressure with an assured authority and devil-may-care dominance in the contests which followed his acquaintance with fame. Within days of completing the post-Indy ticker-tape parade, he was back in action in Wisconsin, and despite a slightly disappointing starting position of tenth on the grid, he powered through the field to attain second place for his fifth consecutive top-five finish in bolstering his reputation as a pillar of reliability, whilst taking the lead – by three points – from his compatriot, Dan Wheldon, in the IRL series.

It was a reminder of the man's maturity and ability to switch from the media glare to the serious business in the blink of an eye. Better still, from the Andretti Green Racing team's perspective, the result in the Milwaukee Mile provided confirmation of just how much improvement Franchitti had

orchestrated since the travails of 2006. Quietly, methodically, he moved into the top five, where he remained for the
majority of the afternoon, and, shrugging off a caution
incurred by one-time leader, Helio Castroneves, the Scot
surged past Wheldon and Sam Hornish, Jnr, in the closing
stages to register a one-two for his employers, with Tony
Kanaan taking the checkered flag, even if the Brazilian driver
must have wished he could have managed that feat on the
previous weekend.

'We expected a slower pace for the race with more stop
and start. It was hard to get positions on the restart with
the heavy traffic, but when we got caught back up, my car
was very good out there,' said Franchitti afterwards, with
a conspicuous determination to allow Kanaan to enjoy his
spell in centre stage. 'We worked very hard at each pit stop
to make it better and, by the end, the car was quite good.'
If the tone of his remarks could hardly have been more
understated, this was Franchitti restored to his natural
habitat: thriving on his quiet man persona, and permitting
the extravagant Kanaan to indulge in the festivities. As both
men privately recognised, the most important feature of the
day was the supremacy which Andretti's organisation was
beginning to exert over its opponents.

That pattern was maintained as June burst out all over
the United States, with the once-diminutive viewing figures
for the IRL showing a marked upturn, the rising numbers
of spectators fuelled by the wall-to-wall coverage of Dario
and Ashley's jig in the Brickyard rain. On the next weekend,
at the Texas Motor Speedway in Fort Worth, Franchitti
recorded fourth place to extend his advantage in the championship to 12 points – over Kanaan – and then he upped
the stakes on the following Sunday with victory in Iowa
which suddenly opened up clear water between him and the
rest of the challengers. In both cases, he had to be both

pragmatic and ruthlessly efficient, a balance which even the leading competitors have occasionally found it hard to strike, but he accomplished it with aplomb. In Texas, he struggled with a variety of problems, and was forced to make a compulsory pit stop as a penalty for coming in under a caution before the pits were open. Where other more volcanic individuals might have reacted with Vesuvian wrath, Franchitti persevered, diligently pursuing points, any amount of points, no matter as long as he continued to chalk up meaningful results, and he gained his reward, coming in behind Hornish Jnr, Kanaan and Danica Patrick. If his post-event assessment was typically concise – 'We lost momentum on the restarts, which was when others really seemed to capitalise, but we also took advantage of some other people's misfortunes [including Dan Wheldon's] and we raced as hard as we could' – the force was flowing in his direction, and there was a semblance of inevitability about the outcome in Iowa.

It wasn't simply that Franchitti transcended all manner of scrapes and smatterings of drama, but also that he seemed capable of rallying from the depths of adversity, whatever the circumstances. Elsewhere, in an accident-packed encounter, there was acrimony and confrontation in the air, but Dario, by deploying the tunnel vision which has always been one of his trademarks, kept out of trouble and remained within the top three for most of the 250-lap event. He skilfully negotiated a multi-car pile-up on lap 99, and applied the coup de grâce when he zoomed past Buddy Rice on lap 151, after a flawless pit stop by his Canadian Club team. Cynics might have retorted that this was akin to chess on four wheels, and that driving ability occasionally seemed less important than Machiavellian strategy, but there was no questioning the efficacy of the Franchitti-led manoeuvres, and when he took on a limited supply of fuel on his final stop, the ploy reaped dividends and he was never in danger of relinquishing his grip on his way to his second win of the season.

It was a formidable display from a fellow at the peak of his powers and, suddenly, he had stacked up a 51-point lead over Kanaan in the championship. Not unnaturally, ebullience coursed through his veins when he spoke to the media later in the day and at least one of the press corps texted me [at a wet cricket ground in Glasgow] with the words: 'Nobody is going to stop this guy!' With hindsight, that was straying into exactly the kind of heightened expectations which Dario was so keen to downplay, but my colleague's faith was justified by the sheer professionalism of the AGR collective. 'It was just a great job by our guys all day. We took a bit of a gamble at the end just to extend our lead, but it worked and it was really fun out there,' said Franchitti, who seemed to be growing tougher the more that he relaxed into the role of favourite, if that isn't a contradiction in terms. 'The car was fantastic and although it was a pretty physical afternoon, it is always terrific coming to Iowa, because this track runs almost like a Superspeedway.'

Even from a distance of a few thousand miles, it was amazing what a remarkable transformation had occurred in the space of a month. At a stroke, the genial team player of the IRL had thrust himself into pole position by the force of his personality and his maturity, and whereas he had been frustrated almost to distraction with inconsistency and glitches in the previous two seasons, here he was in his element and speaking, if not with the quick-fire delivery of an Eddie Murphy or Chris Rock, then certainly with the fluency which made him a natural for the commentary box in the future. 'At first, when I won the Indy 500, it took a little while for it to sink in, because when you have been chasing a prize of that magnitude, there are so many emotions to absorb and you have to step back and soak them all up,' said Franchitti, in the build-up to his triumph in Iowa. 'The bottom line, though, is that the team have been fantastic this season and we have attained the sort of consistency which any driver dreams of, the situation where you expect to be in contention week in, week out, and it is a huge credit to the work which was done during the winter. I thought very early on that we could achieve a lot in this campaign and I could hardly be more happy with the way that things have panned out so far.'

At that juncture, the F1 exploits of Lewis Hamilton had dominated the international motoring headlines for the past month, yet Franchitti's accumulated results, in a far more unpredictable competition, were, if anything, equally impressive. But, perhaps befitting somebody who hadn't so much flirted with danger in the past as invite it upstairs for a Messalina-style encounter, Dario refused to countenance premature celebrations. 'We are heading into a stretch of five consecutive races, which is a hectic schedule in anybody's language, so it will be important to stick to the principles which have taken us this far. But I am really enjoying this season. Iowa is a track which is similar to Pikes Peak and Richmond, both of which are among my favourite circuits, so this should be an exciting period for everybody in the team and we have to be very positive about the future.'

There were few hints yet of the twisty histrionics and clash of wills which would subsequently erupt within the IRL milieu. Instead, the caravan rolled on to Richmond in Virginia with Franchitti in the form of his career and, just as June had commenced, so it climaxed. Once more, there was an insuperable quality to his performance, which denied his challengers even the merest sniff of an opportunity for counter-attack, and the consequence was that Dario powered to his second successive victory, his third of the season, and duly forged a 65-point lead over his nearest rival, Scott

Dixon. In the circumstances, one could understand why Michael Andretti wore the smiling countenance of a man who had just struck the jackpot at Las Vegas, because his driver served up a master class in the fine arts of IRL, starting from pole position, and subsequently pulling away from the rest of the field in much the same fashion the Road Runner used to leave Wile E Coyote clutching at fresh air. A temporary mishap in the pits briefly allowed Tony Kanaan to take the lead after 63 laps, but it was a minor blip and, from the ensuing restart, Franchitti regained the initiative and was never to be troubled again for the remaining 179 laps, in securing his 17th career open-wheel racing victory and his seventh Indy car series triumph. At the death, he was outwardly Arctic-cool, still dampening down any hype, but admitting that he was where he wanted to be in the title battle. None the less, Franchitti possessed too much intelligence and insight into how quickly fortunes could change in his vocation to be lulled into complacency and, once more, amidst the euphoria of his technicians and mechanics, he claimed that he believed the IRL joust would continue until the very last race on the calendar. At that stage, even he must have hoped that he could avoid such a scenario, but Franchitti's prescience was justified, not only because Dixon, who finished second, was showing signs of launching a sustained challenge to his Scottish opponent, but also in light of the little tremors and flickers of temperament which were evident in Andretti's make-up. One could have supposed the latter would bask in the limelight, but as somebody whose son was also involved in the competition, he had previously shown a tendency to stoke controversy in public, rather than adopting the Sir Alex Ferguson philosophy of keeping arguments and spats confined to the dressing room. In which light, Richmond was the last time the AGR squad could afford to relax. Thereafter, as June drifted into July, there were more detours and disruptions than anybody wanted.

'I enjoy driving at Richmond a lot. I think it suits my style, because you have to feel what the car is doing and react to it. The Canadian Club guys have given me really good cars here, so that obviously makes my job a little bit easier, and the engineering staff at AGR were really on the top of their game,' said Franchitti. 'We took some big gambles to get on pole last night, and my engineer, Allen McDonald, took an educated guess today, and it worked out just fine for us.' His demeanour was sunny, his disposition relaxed, and several commentators dashed into print, proclaiming Dario as champion, even though the IRL didn't conclude until September. But it was far too early to engage in grand-standing gestures, let alone contemplate a coronation, as the Scot discovered to his cost.

All the same, there were scant grounds for trepidation when the action switched to Watkins Glen in New York. Granted, Franchitti had to settle for third, albeit it was his ninth straight top-five result, behind Dixon and Sam Hornish, Jnr, but he still produced an efficient display and harassed and harried his opponents from the outset. Indeed, he attempted to overtake the New Zealand competitor on the very first lap, narrowly avoiding making contact with the Chip Ganassi vehicle, and that set the tone for a furious and frenetic tussle between racers who knew each other's strengths and weaknesses inside out. Dario advanced into second when Helio Castroneves spun out of control, sparking the first caution of the event, but he slipped back to tenth, following the second round of pit stops, where several drivers elected to continue without refuelling. It was clear that some of AGR's adversaries had adapted their strategies in response to the ease with which Franchitti had romped home in Richmond, and their ploys paid off to a significant extent.

At the halfway point, Dario moved up to eighth, but still had to battle his way through slower traffic, which dashed any prospects of him pursuing another victory. However, he did manage to progress up the standings, eventually passing team mate, Marco Andretti, with only ten laps remaining, and if the afternoon could scarcely be described as an aesthetic treat, the outcome kept Franchitti 47 points in front of Dixon, even if there were signs that the younger man had clawed back a fair amount of momentum. 'I think second place was what we were really hoping for, but we lost a little bit of time in the pits and that eventually proved the difference between second and third,' said Franchitti. 'I am not unhappy, because it was a very, very tough race. In fact, to be honest, it was maybe one of the toughest. I am just going to keep fighting Scott for the championship and I have the feeling that it will go down to the wire, because he is the strongest guy in the points right now. But hopefully, we can do something about that.'

That candour was typical of Franchitti's insistent refusal to count chickens, but the pressure increased on the Andretti brigade in the weeks ahead, sparking some bird-brained outbursts from people at the summit of the organisation, who would surely have been wiser to have kept their counsel. Perhaps the angst had been provoked by reports, as yet unsubstantiated, that the Scot was poised to enter into talks with Ganassi over the prospect of joining the NASCAR ranks. Or maybe it was simply that Michael Andretti couldn't properly distinguish the difference between being manager and cheer-leader. But, whatever the reason, slippage and sloppiness crept into the team's efforts.

That, of course, shouldn't detract from the sterling qualities of Dixon, who wrested control of the championship throughout July and August and hunted down Franchitti with the tenacity and relentlessness of Jack Bauer, minus the torture. First up, amidst the good ol' Southern lieges at the Nashville Superspeedway, he survived a torrid test of character with Dario to restrict the Scot to second place, then, the following week, history repeated itself at the Mid-Ohio Sports Car Course, as the IRL was transformed into a two-man band. Both slugged it out for a couple of hours in Tennessee, the pair exhibiting the kind of bravura initiatives and visceral manoeuvres which had captivated the sport's enthusiasts, but although Dario strove manfully to disrupt his opponent's rhythm, he couldn't quite achieve what had seemed so elementary earlier in the season. 'We just got screwed up in traffic all day,' was Franchitti's response to coming second in Nashville. And that problem resurfaced in Lexington a week later, where Dario, starting the race from fifth position, was consistently quicker than the leader, but found himself with limited opportunities to accelerate into the territory where he might have been capable of tracing a route past Dixon. 'Second place would have been okay, if it wasn't for the fact Scott was in front of us again,' he said later, in the knowledge that his IRL lead had been trimmed to just 24 points. 'He really drove a great race and so did Helio Castroneves as well. We were pushing against one another the whole time, or as much as our cars would allow, and it was quite a battle. I know that it is going to be like this until the end of the championship, but I was never expecting anything else and we simply have to put our heads down and get ready for the challenge. We kind of messed up at the start, because we had 'Dixie' (Dixon) covered, but then Danica [Patrick] slid, Tony [Kanaan] spun whilst trying to avoid her, and then Marco [Andretti] also got involved. I had to check up to avoid getting wiped out by Tony and that stacked up a lot of the problems for us right there, but these sort of things happen in racing and you just have to get on with it.'

Less diplomatic characters than Franchitti might have questioned why the AGR drivers seemed to be working against one another, rather than for the greater good of the one man in their ranks who could actually win the title. But it wasn't and had never been in Dario's nature to live according to an Ayrton Senna or Michael Schumacher and go searching for scapegoats and become embroiled in punch-ups and verbal disputes at the climax of these testosterone-charged battles. Could that be considered a fault? I once asked Sir Jackie Stewart that question and his response was as measured as it was sensible. 'When you are out there on the track, you have to push yourself to the limit and you have to keep your emotions in check, otherwise you are putting yourself and those around you in danger. Of course, when a race finishes and you feel you have a grievance with a colleague or a rival, you are entitled to raise the issue, but I don't think it does anybody any good to start screaming and looking for fights. Because, at the end of the day, we are all human, we all make mistakes, and most of us, if we have the right values, are prepared to put our hands up when we have got it wrong.' In short, Franchitti could have lapsed into McEnroe-style madness or raged at x, y or z, but he knew that he too would mess up sooner or later. And, in the wider picture, what mattered was how you dealt with adversity as much as how you basked in the moment of triumph.

The validity of that message was emphasised in the most graphic manner imaginable on the next stretch of the IRL marathon when the motorcade pulled into Brooklyn for the Firestone Indy 400. There was nothing in the preliminaries or in the activities of the other participants to deflect attention away from *the* talking point of the contest, which persuaded hundreds of thousands of worldwide internet users to witness for themselves the utterly terrifying, late-race incident which might easily have ended Franchitti's life. Indeed, nine months after the accident, I logged on to the YouTube site to watch it again – despite feeling queasy about the motivation which compels so many human beings to derive what I regard as vicarious pleasure or schadenfreude from surveying these near-death experiences at a safe distance – and still found myself rubbing my eyes in disbelief. Not merely at the sanguine fashion in which Franchitti picked himself up and climbed back into the cockpit less than a week later, but at the cool-as-Antarctica manner in which he discussed the whole thing during Larry King's CNN programme shortly after being propelled into mid-air at 250mph.

In prosaic terms, these drivers have to possess a reflex mechanism, whereby they can shrug aside such 'mishaps' (one of the euphemisms employed in the aftermath), but, if we disregard the stiff upper lip routinely deployed on these occasions, this was the equivalent of bungee-jumping towards the old man with the scythe – and, incidentally, something which served to vindicate the belief held by many of us that these particular sportsmen's salaries are justified. A few hours after staring at oblivion in Michigan, Franchitti's immediate response was one of understandable relief. 'When I went upside down, I thought that was it, but then I hit [Scott] Dixon on the way down and I have to thank him, because he definitely softened the blow. I talked to Dan [Wheldon] about it and he bobbed when I weaved and we just got together,' he told a group of incredulous journalists, most of whom rarely have to face anything more terrifying than having their expenses invest-igated. 'I do want to see a replay of it, though. I did think at one stage when I was flying upwards: 'Hmm, this isn't good.' But the Canadian Club car was really good today and that was positive.'

This was in the spirit of Douglas Bader or Malcolm Campbell: a refusal to be cowed or intimidated by circumstances which would appal the average person. Even when pressed on the issue by the beetle-browed King, a chap who has grilled and barbecued some of the most famous personalities on the geopolitical and artistic stage, Dario remained the embodiment of stoicism. Asked why he was still alive, he replied: 'I had some luck, for sure. But a lot of time and effort has gone into making Indy cars and all types of race cars safer through the years. I definitely think I owe my life to the people that have made those advances and somebody was definitely looking out for me there.'

He went on: 'I had no injuries, apart from a little bit of bruising on the nose. That's about it. I was actually able to go to the gym on Monday morning and I felt no ill effects at all. I really can't believe it. But, as you will understand, I am not complaining about it, either.'

KING: 'What caused the accident?'

FRANCHITTI: 'The accident was caused, in my opinion, by the car next to me moving up the track into the back of my car. I think it was a misjudgement by Dan Wheldon, who was driving the other vehicle. I don't believe he did it on purpose, far from it, but I just believe it was a slight misjudgement and that was the result. The regulations have something to do with it as well, because on these types of tracks, we run very, very close together, and that means that there is zero margin for error. And we saw the result.'

KING: 'Why do you race cars, Dario?'

FRANCHITTI: 'I do it because I love it. I've done it nearly all my life – I've raced karts since I was ten years old and I have wanted to be a racing driver since I was four. I know that danger is a part of the sport and it is not a part of the sport that I enjoy. I lost my best friend [Greg Moore] to an accident in 1999, but I accept the risks, because I love the job that I do and I would not be involved in it if that wasn't the case.'

KING: 'Is this a sport that is teachable?'

FRANCHITTI: 'You can teach people so much, but there has to be some natural instinct involved. Jackie Stewart is always talking about mind management and making the mind work as well as it can for you. And, although we travel at such tremendous speeds, everything happens almost in slow motion. So, in some ways, it is akin to golf, in that you have to get your mind working in the right way as well as everything else.'

KING: 'What was going through your mind when the car was going up in the air?'

FRANCHITTI: 'Well, as soon as the car kicked sideways – and you have to remember this was the first time I had been upside down in a 24-year career – as soon as it kicked sideways, I felt . . . the first thought was that this is not good.'

KING: 'Good thinking.'

FRANCHITTI: 'And then, when it went upside down, I opened my eyes again as the car was travelling backwards and at that point I felt OK, but wondered how bad it was going to be. You ask yourself in a split second: "How bad is it going to hurt and what's going to break and how bad is the concussion going to be?", because I have suffered a few of these injuries in the past, mostly not driving Indy cars. And then, when I hit the ground, I couldn't believe how small the impact was. When the car finally came to a rest, I was just amazed that I was still in one piece and pretty thankful for being so.'

KING: 'What does Ashley think of your profession?'

FRANCHITTI: 'She loves my profession. She loves coming to the races and she is a really big race fan. Since she met me, she has really grown to love the sport and I think it's more difficult for her a lot of the time – and that goes for my family, my mom, my dad, my sister, my brother – to watch sometimes than it is for me to do it.'

KING: 'Did she see the accident on Sunday?'

FRANCHITTI: 'You know it worked out very well. She was watching the race at home and she had gone outside to fill the bird feeder up. And then she came back inside and saw that I was getting out of the car, which was in pieces. So she got to see the replay, already knowing that I was okay. And that was something else to be thankful for.'

KING: 'Video of the crash is available on YouTube.com and, according to the current figures, at least 250,000 people have tuned in to watch it. Why do you think that so many of us are fascinated with watching crashes like that?'

FRANCHITTI: 'I'm not sure what is in the human mind that enjoys it. I have to say that I don't enjoy watching them myself. Yes, I watched the replay, but I only did so because I wanted to know how the accident started. I don't enjoy watching my own accidents and I don't enjoy watching other people's either, whatever the sport may be, because, you know, I think I have been in so many myself that I know what it is like.'

Dario's answers were indicative of the lessons he had learned from a career embracing almost every positive and negative. The reference to Moore, for instance, demonstrated that his late confrère remained very much in Franchitti's thoughts, while his bemusement as to why so many ghoulish individuals should be obsessed with endlessly watching pictures of mayhem and destruction testified to the very humanity which is lacking in these people. What shone through in his conversation with King was his grounded attitude to matters of life and death and his down-to-earth perspective on his priorities, allied to an appreciation that some features of motor-sport are outwith anybody's control. It was as well that he had adopted this approach, because the next steps on his path in pursuit of the IRL championship would test his resolve, his courage and his patience to the limit.

9

A SCRIPT STRAIGHT FROM HOLLYWOOD

As the clock ticked down on the Indy Racing League and the joust between Dario Franchitti and Scott Dixon assumed a relentless momentum, it became impossible to forecast which of the couple would finish with the title in his grasp. Occasionally in sport, these personal duels within a team context are the most captivating elements of the business – one instantly thinks of Andrew Flintoff tormenting Jacques Kallis with a mesmerising spell of fast bowling at Edgbaston in the summer of 2008, or the peerless Jonny Wilkinson kicking the stuffing out of the Australians during the 2003 Rugby World Cup final – and thus it proved on the Indy circuit as summer lapsed into early autumn.

It wasn't simply that Dixon kept nibbling away at his opponent's lead, but also that Franchitti's hitherto impressive decision-making seemed to desert him for a period. With hindsight, considering how he had been shaken up by the crash in Michigan, it was an impressive display of courage that he should return to the competitive fray less than a week later on August 11 at the Kentucky Speedway circuit in Sparta. But this was not one of his more memorable outings, with his eight-place finish allowing Dixon, who ended as runner-up behind Kanaan, to trim Franchitti's advantage to just eight points. Dario consistently ran in the top three for most of the race, and led for 52 laps, but while entering the pit lane for his final stop on lap 179, he bumped into a cone and was forced to change the front wing of his Canadian Club vehicle. From there, there was nothing else but for him to accept, with a mixture of resignation and annoyance, that he would have to settle for one of the minor placings, and yet his afternoon worsened with another chilling reminder of how the most innocuous incidents can sometimes have potentially dreadful consequences. As he crossed the finish line, Franchitti inadvertently made contact with Kosuke Matsuura, which sent the Scot's car airborne in yet another terrifying end-over-end flip. At first glance, there was a numb sense of consternation amongst his team and a substantial section of the crowd which witnessed the crash, whose silence amounted to the collective thought: 'Surely, he can't be as lucky as he was last time around.' But thankfully, although his car sustained a considerable amount of damage, Franchitti walked away uninjured, virtually without a scratch, from the wreckage.

It was little surprise that he should concentrate less on the result than counting his blessings, but he immediately shouldered the responsibility and acknowledged that events had spiralled out of control. 'It was my fault, no question about it. I heard "checkered" just as I hit Kosuke and I want to apologise to him. That was my second mistake of the race and it could have been a big one.' Franchitti's equanimity was not shared by his race strategist, John Anderson, who was clearly growing rattled at the manner in which Dixon was closing the gap, apparently inexorably, on the AGR ensemble. 'Dario went high, coming out of Turn 4, and lost a number of positions. Then we collected a cone coming into the pits and that caused us fresh problems. We really need to get back into the swing of things as championship contenders and we need to do it soon.'

However, the tensions within the organisation were already conspicuous and the bust-up which had always threatened to explode, given the volatility of the Andrettis, duly occurred within the Infineon Speedway at Sonoma in California, where Franchitti relinquished the IRL lead for the first time since June. There was little hint of the drama in store as Dario began the race in magisterial fashion, securing the lead for 22 laps as the prelude to the first round of green-flag pit stops. After these had been completed, he continued in much the same dominant vein and, for a considerable period, it genuinely appeared that he had returned to the imperious form which had marked his earlier displays. But suddenly, with only a dozen laps remaining, and with a sorely-required victory in his grasp, Franchitti made slight contact with Marco Andretti, which caused damage to the Scot's front wing, and that brought a full-course caution. Even then, Dario stayed on the track in a desperate attempt to carry on scrapping for the win, but he was unable to climb any higher than third in a frantic climax, whilst Dixon sped to success and punched the air with an unusually flamboyant gesture of delight. Elsewhere, though, there was a starkly contrasting mood among the AGR drivers. Initially, at least, Franchitti sought to sound rational and cool-headed. 'The day was going really well for us, until Marco and I got together. Tony and I had a similar situation on the stop before that and TK opened up the door and gave me the room I needed, but I really want to look at what happened with Marco and have a talk with him. We are team-mates. We have to look after each other and that kind of thing shouldn't be happening. We will have it out.'

But, as matters transpired, this was a row which couldn't be settled behind closed doors. Dixon, normally as unflappable a customer as Franchitti, was furious in the aftermath, claiming he had been victimised by 'team tactics' from the AGR squad and adding that the rival team had 'got what they deserved' during the denouement. 'Today was very frustrating, especially having to deal with Kanaan, who was not playing fair at all,' declared Dixon. 'We were all warned in the drivers' meetings about team tactics and I think the IRL authorities must have been watching another race, because it was definitely going on out there. That is why it was kind of ironic when Dario and Marco hit each other. I could see it all happening in front of me. Marco was coming out of the pits and Dario was at full speed. Dario probably thought that because Marco was his team-mate, he was obviously going to give him some room. But I really don't think Marco knew he was there and it felt like karma when the pair of them ended up in a tangle.'

Unsurprisingly, Dixon felt inclined to stoke the flames, observing that this had been the sixth successive race where he had earned more points than Franchitti. 'That is clearly going to create a bit of investigation within their ranks and bring a lot of stress.' He was correct. Barely had the dust settled before Dario and Marco were explaining their sides of the story, whilst Michael Andretti responded as if he had been stung by a wasp. 'Dario should have shown more patience,' said the owner, signalling where he believed the blame should lie. As for Marco himself, he claimed, rather naively, that he was only interested in pursuing victories, instead of being preoccupied with the larger picture. 'I gave racing room and I was hoping that Dario would race me clean. I hate to think he would do anything [wrong] intentionally. I was saving so much fuel and my car was good enough that we were still catching them as we were saving fuel and that would have been the win in the pocket. If we had played fair, that is what would have happened.'

It was an undignified affair, but symptomatic of the tensions which were now evident, not only between Andretti and Franchitti, but also the former and Chip Ganassi, the owner of Dixon's CGR team, who was famously described by one American commentator as being 'as lovable as a punch in the face'. Non-motoring enthusiasts might have concluded that the couple deserved one another, given their dual capacity for sparking controversy and clamour wherever they ventured, but as subsequent events unfolded, it was evident the duo got on about as happily as Michael Moore and George Bush.

Naturally, the tension had started to affect both the leading team owners, and with two races remaining on the calendar, a miasma of ill-feeling hung over the IRL series as the drivers arrived in Detroit at the beginning of September. This Indy Grand Prix was an event in which Franchitti had to reassert his authority, otherwise he would be staring at a repeat of the anti-climactic conclusion of 1999. To his credit, he refused to buckle under the pressure. Once again, as in the previous contests, the afternoon was packed with incidents, contentious clashes and the sort of adrenaline-charged performances from the protagonists which guaranteed a scintillating tussle and plenty of acrimony in the aftermath. Starting from second place on the grid, Dario exuded calmness while waiting in Helio Castroneves' slipstream until the first round of pit stops, but subsequently snatched the lead on lap 27 and gradually increased his advantage, prior to making his second stop on lap 50, at which stage he found he had slipped to fifth, because three of his competitors had elected to stay out on the circuit. It was at best a debatable strategy, at worst, a ploy which threatened to explode in Franchitti's face, but he maintained his charge and with just over 20 laps to go, the fifth full-course caution came out and matters descended into a bizarre mêlée as the finish beckoned. Dario decided to take fuel only on what would be the last stop, but as the different teams settled on a variety of tactics, he endured all manner of conflicting emotions in a slightly surreal half-hour period. For a spell, he seemed to have grabbed the ascendancy, masterfully passing A J Foyt IV and Danica Patrick to move into fourth, narrowly behind Tony Kanaan, Buddy Rice and Scott Dixon, but it was at this juncture that one or two participants flung their teddies out of the pram and sparked a ruckus. With just one lap left, Rice and Dixon made contact, Franchitti was caught up in the collision and the consequence was that Dixon suffered serious damage to his vehicle, which allowed his rival to gain the upper hand by continuing through to the checkered flag in sixth spot, with victory for Kanaan – his fifth of the season – almost an irrelevance as tempers boiled over in the post-mortem.

For his part, Franchitti was simply content that destiny was again in his own hands and that if he finished ahead of Dixon in the finale, he would be the champion. 'The Canadian Club car was very fast today, and when we were running behind Helio, we were able to save fuel, which was a definite bonus. But then we got in traffic and couldn't make anything happen and it was very difficult to get past anybody out there. We were posting lap times up to three seconds faster than some of those in front of us, but we couldn't get past and it does get frustrating. Then, towards the end, Buddy ran out of fuel and Scott made contact with him, spun around and collected me in the process. To my knowledge, no yellow flag had been given, so the safety guys couldn't come on to the track to help me reverse and get back into gear, so I was just sitting there for a while. It was a crazy day, but the important thing is that we have regained the lead in the IRL and we have to capitalise on that next week.'

As analyses go, this was sober, honest and measured. Everything in fact that was alien to Andretti, who responded to the action in Detroit by confronting Chip Ganassi and accusing his driver, Dixon, of intentionally backing into Franchitti's path after the New Zealand driver's mistake on the last lap. 'Poor sportsmanship is what I saw. Dixon clearly took Dario out on purpose. He was rolling and going fine and then he saw Dario was going to the outside of him, let off his brake, and took Dario out. It was totally on purpose and I am really disappointed in Scott,' said Andretti, with kettlefuls of steam still emerging from his ears. 'He can claim what he likes and I guess that we can't prove it was a deliberate act. But, you know, after what he said about us last weekend, this proves that what goes round comes around. He has lost the lead and he won't be confident now.'

This might have carried more validity if his opinion had been echoed by Franchitti or if Dixon's transgression had brought him some tangible reward. But neither was true. On the contrary, Dario was able to keep his engine fired and make it through to sixth, whereas Dixon was only credited with eighth position, which was enough of a gap for the Scot, who led the most laps, to climb to the summit of the standings by a slender margin of three points. And he refused to make his challenger any sort of scapegoat. 'I don't think that Scott did anything on purpose. He went for a gap when Buddy ran out of fuel, he spun, he was going left and going right and I chose the wrong way and he rolled back as I was going in that direction,' said Franchitti. 'It was just unfortunate, but these kind of things happen when you are pushing yourself to the margins. Sometimes, you can't do right for doing wrong, but it was a weird day and I have no problem with Scott.'

Elsewhere, though, Kanaan, who had not even been involved in the incident, shared Andretti's stance with a paranoia which would have appealed to the Lone Gunmen from *The X Files* or the conspiracy theorists who clog up the internet with their delusional ravings on everything from how 'Capricorn One' was the literal truth to their contention that the 9/11 World Trade Center tragedy was orchestrated by the Bush administration to shore up the president's poor personal ratings. 'I will never be Scott Dixon, but after all the heat that he gave me last weekend . . . well, let's just say the guy didn't believe me when I tried to defend myself at Sonoma. So you will have to read into that what you will,' said the Brazilian. 'But the bottom line is he has lost the championship lead, I guess that he won't be sleeping very well this week and I am coming [for him].'

In this inflamed atmosphere, it was understandable that some American commentators, even those usually immune to these puerile descents into playground fights, were shocked by the level of vitriol being aimed at the mild-mannered Dixon and his owner, Ganassi. 'Catch Chip at a bad time and he will go out of his way to be a wise guy in an attempt to embarrass you for asking what he thinks is a smart-ass question,' remarked ESPN's columnist, Bruce Martin. 'Let's face it, he is like the kid in high school, who always had a way of annoying you the most. He was the one you would love to snap your towel at after gym class.' And yet Michael Andretti and [fellow AGR team owner] Kevin Savoree are turning Ganassi into a sympathetic figure.'

'I think Michael and Kevin over-reacted to what they saw on television, which happens,' said Mike Hull, the managing director of Target CGR Racing. 'What I thought was lacking in class was the way they treated Mr Ganassi. I won't repeat what they said, but they should understand that Buddy Rice ran out of fuel and Scott had nowhere to go. They accused

Chip of ordering him to take Dario out. But we don't race like that and it is too bad that they react in the way that they do. I think that it is a pretty classless way for adults to behave. Kevin was trying to get Chip to take a swing at him, but Chip didn't bite.'

Bruce Martin summed up the situation astutely in these terms: 'At Infineon, it was Andretti who was upset at Franchitti, after he knocked his son, Marco, out of the way. At that point, Andretti went from being Franchitti's team owner to Marco's "Little League Dad." Now, the frustration is being directed at his fellow Pennsylvanian, Ganassi. But, instead of being a battle of these two natives of the Keystone State, Andretti and Savoree looked more like the Keystone Cops after confronting The Mighty Chip. At the same time, the Andretti attitude has brought this year's IndyCar title to a new level of intensity which has made this season far more interesting than the weekly stock-car snore-a-thons [of the rival NASCAR circuit]. But who would ever have imagined that it would be possible to make Ganassi a lovable character and a sympathetic personality?'

In the event, though, such considerations were far from Franchitti's mind when he climbed into his car at the Chicagoland Speedway on September 9. All the petty verbals, the theatrical language and Dick Dastardly-style stage whispers counted for nothing in the hard currency of results and Franchitti was old and wise enough to appreciate that nobody would recall his identity if he wound up in the role of gallant loser. Yet for much of the proceedings, that seemed the probable fate for Dario as he battled to extract a competitive performance from a vehicle which seemed strangely off the pace. Starting from pole position, he had the ideal platform to dictate the tempo, lay down a declaration of intent to Dixon and, or so he might have assumed, sail off into the distance. Yet, even from the opening laps of the event, which commanded a massive worldwide audience – a testament to the manner in which the IRL had finally caught fire outside the United States – Franchitti was forced to languish down the field, slipping down to fourth and fifth, and looking visibly strained as the intensity of the battle heightened. The only equation which was of any consequence was the fact that he had to finish in front of Dixon to claim the title. For long stretches, however, such an outcome appeared distinctly unlikely, with the New Zealand man seizing the initiative and the lead for the majority of the contest.

As the laps passed, a horrible sense of déjà vu nagged away at Franchitti's resolve. Almost a decade after his grim struggle with Juan Pablo Montoya, was this another illustration of how he was the nearly man when he wasn't being the invisible man? But he could at least derive comfort from the sheer unpredictability of the campaign, and the way in which both drivers had endured a maelstrom of conflicting sentiments and sensations, stretching considerably further than Hepburn's early gamut of emotions. 'For most of the race, I couldn't do anything. I couldn't pass the guys in front, because they were running side by side and it was imperative that I didn't do anything rash. There were times when the car wasn't handling well, and I had just had to hang on, I had to focus on the positives, and remember how I got into the position to win the championship in the first place,' said Franchitti, who careered towards the climax, still in touch, but with his chances hanging by a thread. 'Eventually, people were pitting and we all had to keep reassessing our tactics. Dan [Wheldon] ran out of fuel, and it was just Scott and I, and as we headed towards the conclusion, it was only Scott and I on the lead lap, but he was in front and, for a while, it looked as if that was going to be the crucial factor.'

It was sensational, white-knuckle, edge-of-the-seat entertainment, and after seven months, 16 races and 198 laps of the decisive Peak Antifreeze 300, the title had boiled down to a fight between two individuals and two teams gambling on fuel strategy and sweating over which of the pair could outlast the other. Such a scenario had been generated on lap 137, when Vitor Meira had crashed into the Turn Four wall – he emerged unscathed – necessitating an extended yellow caution, which allowed both Franchitti and Dixon to top off their fuel supply on lap 147, placing them on a separate tactical path from the rest of the field. It still appeared that both men would have to make a final stop for one small splash of fuel, but at almost the same moment on lap 195, the hapless Wheldon pulled up on the backstretch, and Danica Patrick spun out. The subsequent caution provided the leaders with the option of going for broke, without having any more business in the pits. This was it: no more nonsense, no more bullshit from the owners, nothing but a titanic tussle between two humans. The race went green for a climactic two-lap shoot-out, with Dario vying for supremacy, snapping at Dixon's tail, but unable to orchestrate the coup de grâce. For a few seconds, both vehicles were virtually side by side, and there was even the faint prospect of a dead heat, which would have ensured Franchitti secured the title. Then, once more, Dixon edged ahead, and, as the Scot had forecast months before, destiny had arrived not at the eleventh hour, but with the clock reading 11.59.59 and Dario on the verge of turning into a pumpkin.

By this juncture, many of us could hardly dare to watch. It wasn't even as if Dixon could be turned into some kind of hate figure, considering the man's genial nature and the knowledge that his lofty estimation of Franchitti was reciprocated by the latter. But patriotism can do strange things to the most reserved of customers and suddenly, even when it seemed impossible that anything could deny Dixon as he entered Turn Three on the final lap, his vehicle spluttered, his fuel supply ran out, and he ground almost to a halt. It all occurred with such swiftness that Franchitti nearly crashed into his adversary, but he managed to swerve past the gap and sped to the checkered flag as the precursor to a massive outpouring of joy from every single member of the AGR organisation.

Here was vindication for years of toil, redemption after a painful catalogue of near-misses with success and even sorer collisions with reality, gravity and roads from Scotland to the United States. No wonder that Franchitti, usually a model citizen, was overcome by the magnitude of what he had just achieved, and hugged anybody who came within distance, as he raced around the engineers, technicians, team-mates, the sprinkling of Scots in the audience, and punched the air with the unalloyed delight of somebody who had just won his first senior title since 1993. 'I am stunned. That was a hell of a finish, just about unbelievable. But there again, maybe we shouldn't have expected anything else, given how the season has panned out. But it was some good strategy by my boys on the team and I will go and thank every one of them personally as soon as I can.' His whose words carried a valedictory air, because he knew he would soon be bidding adieu to the AGR crew, in pursuit of a new challenge in the NASCAR ranks. 'It has been a great campaign, a terrific battle from start to finish and I can't really explain how overjoyed I feel. But I have loved working with all my guys and racing in front of these fantastic IndyCar fans and I want to soak up the atmosphere and breathe it in, because this is a special moment for me.'

In the ensuing period, one of the most conspicuous features was the simpatico between the two characters whose lives had become inextricably intertwined on the IRL quest. 'I just don't think that Dario's car was as quick today as the Penske cars and those of Dan and myself, but that shows you how he got stuck in and kept scrapping away and he never ever gives up,' said Dixon. 'Midway through the race, we knew we had a very good chance of winning the championship, but going into the final restart, I knew it was going to be incredibly close and he went past me when it mattered. Obviously, I am a little disappointed at the moment, but I reckon Dario is a great competitor, and, to be honest, if anybody else had to win the title, I am glad it was him, given how he has refused to let things get to him and how he has been totally focused on this objective.'

Certainly, Franchitti's best qualities had surfaced in adversity. His resilience, his patience and refusal to buckle after relinquishing a 65-point advantage were all commendable, even before one recalls the circumstances in which he had transcended brushes with his Maker as if they were mere piffling obstacles, comparable to rush-hour traffic jams or 'Out of Order' signs at the petrol pump. In bare statistical terms, Franchitti led for 718 laps in 2007 compared with Dixon's tally of 291. There had been a miscommunication with Marco Andretti, a brief contretemps with his father, Michael, and a range of gremlins in abject August which were as aggravating as the experiences of May and June had been a source of delight. On this decisive visit to Chicago, he had frequently looked off the pace, he had trailed in grim pursuit without possessing the requisite acceleration to contemplate gaining the upper hand. Lesser mortals might have slumped into petulance, but as Franchitti absorbed the implications of his triumph, he was both rational and jubilant, with a hint of serenity in the realisation he would no longer have to justify himself to anybody, or survey his career with a sense of recherché du temps perdu.

'Sometimes, I get a little bit hot under the collar, but I was very calm in the car all day at the Chicagoland. As hard as I was trying, I couldn't make anything happen, but the one thing I knew I could do was save fuel and that helped us at the finish, didn't it? The most important thing for me was to drive a good race and give it 100 per cent, because you can't really improve on that. I did the job my guys wanted me to do and that was actually more important to me than the result. I don't know if it's because I won the Indy 500 and that took some of the pressure off my shoulders, but I was pretty relaxed today. I know that Scott is a terrific driver, and I had to aim to hang on to his coat-tails, but we have gone through a lot this season and nobody can take this away from us.' Franchitti refused to be drawn on the question of his impending exit from the IRL ranks, in advance of the official confirmation of his move to Chip Ganassi's NASCAR organisation, but he was perfectly happy to discuss what he regarded as the pivotal moments in a campaign where he had tasted every nuance of pleasure and pain, on his way to four race triumphs [he was equal with Dixon, while Kanaan won five, but proved less consistent over the whole course]. 'The biggest mental challenge this year was jumping back into the car in Kentucky, five days after flipping the car in Michigan, but to get over that barrier . . . well, I thought, if I can do that, I can handle anything else thrown at me.

'Don't get me wrong, I appreciate that I have been lucky this season. Some things could have turned out differently. Very differently. For a while, people kept asking me: "Is this good luck going to continue? Is this good luck going to continue?" And one of my friends said to me the other day: "Did you expect this season to be so perfect?" But you know, I have suffered other times where nothing has gone right and it is how you respond to these various situations which makes the difference. Of course, winning the Indy 500 was fabulous and it provided a launch pad. Does it overshadow the rest of the season? Yeah, to some extent, it does.

But there is also something to be said for being the person who does the best on all different types of tracks, especially since the street courses have been introduced and now we have them and short ovals and two-milers and all these other circuits. So you have got to get it right, week in, week out, and you can't afford to be one-dimensional in this sport. You have to keep testing yourself, pushing yourself, and I am extremely proud of the fact that all the Canadian Club racing guys did that.'

In the next few days, Franchitti and his family celebrated privately, embodying the collectivism which had guided the son to his triumph. Stirling Moss once defined Jackie Stewart as 'the man who drove fast enough to win at the lowest possible speed,' and there was something similarly under-stated about the relationship between Dario and George. Yes, they were – and remain – pragmatic figures, but there has always been a constant desire to soak up information and absorb knowledge like human ink blotters. Even as they toasted the IRL victory with Marina, Marino, Ashley and the Di Resta clan, it was evident that the gruelling journey from West Lothian to West of Hollywood had been more than worthwhile; it had demonstrated the power of family ties and close-knit bonds, immutably cemented at an early age and strengthened thereafter. Nobody had ever put Dario under any pressure to become obsessed with cars and motor-sport, but from the time he had been knee-high to a grasshopper, he had been champing to go faster and faster. Those American commentators who interviewed him in his hours of glory marvelled at the poise with which he reacted to success. As a youngster, he had been instructed that you had to be ruthless to succeed in the business, but Dario had never sacrificed his dignity or decency in the process, if for no other reason than that George had been with him almost every step of the journey. And, as somebody close to them told me: 'This can be a very lonely sport without the support of your nearest and dearest, because from the first time you ever go to a karting event, you will be in there with a hundred other sets of fathers and sons and they all want to kick your backside and they all realise that only one or two of the youngsters will ever get anywhere near the top. So it is hellishly competitive and it can develop into situations where some people behave like complete arseholes. You have the really pushy parents, the ones who aren't happy unless they are falling out with everybody else at the circuit and screaming blue murder at anybody who they think is trying to muck around with their wee lad, and, basically, being in that environment can destroy the good part of people's natures. Over the course of ten years, George and Dario Franchitti came at the racing from a different angle. They travelled thousands of miles together to meetings all over Britain, went further afield to Europe when they had the chance and then, even when Dario journeyed to the United States, George would be over in America as often as he possibly could be, cheering on and encouraging the boys, staying in the background, but letting the two of them – because he has shown the same amount of dedication to Marino – know that he was always there, always supportive, without ever wanting to be in the limelight.'

This has been a recurring theme in Dario's story, a commitment to compartmentalising the truly significant things in his existence. Naturally, he was jubilant in the aftermath of the dramatic events in Chicago, but sadness soon intruded on the joie de vivre. Which brings us to a late Thursday afternoon in September in the south of England, where Sir Jackie Stewart was mulling over questions of mortality and inwardly shedding a tear. Normally a little coiled spring of unfettered optimism and Micawberish positivity, the veteran world champion, who had revelled in Franchitti's IRL triumph, was in contemplative mood, having just attended the funeral of his rallying compatriot, Colin McRae, killed in a helicopter accident along with his son, Johnny, and two other passengers, close to the pilot's home in Lanarkshire. Understandably, the proceedings were shrouded in the grief of three families, and even Stewart, whose career had regularly alternated between champagne-laced podium celebrations and lachrymose memorial services, seemed perplexed as to how sportsmen such as McRae and the former Isle of Man TT champion, Steve Hislop, can flirt with danger at 200mph during hazard-strewn races and emerge unscathed from the pitfalls, only to perish upon entering retirement. 'It happened to Graham Hill [who was killed in an air crash in 1975], it happened to Steve Hislop and now it has happened to Colin, who was no frivolous risk-taker. It is very difficult to get your head round it. I mean, here was somebody who had been the most exuberant, on-the-limit driver in the business and he had survived all kinds of accidents, and suddenly we were standing in the church and there was Colin's wife [Alison] and daughter [Holly] and all the other victims' families, and there was this awful sense of desolation and loss. God works in strange ways, doesn't he? I talked to Dario Franchitti at the funeral and he was reflecting on how he had suffered two enormous crashes this season, where his car had catapulted through the air, and yet he was able to walk away from both of them with barely a scratch. It makes you think about fate and what might be waiting round the corner, and it forces all of us to understand that you can attempt to control as many pieces of your life as you possibly can, but there are always elements which are outwith your control and nobody has all the answers.

'When I was in Formula One, yes, there were tragedies, and far too many of them, but the drivers were doing what they wanted to do and we were all aware of the dangers involved in the sport. At that stage [in the 1960s and 1970s] I always believed there was a little pouch, close to my chest, next to my heart, which would help to dilute the grief. Yet, as I have grown older, I have recognised that because of the number of occasions when [his wife] Helen and I have been confronted with death, the little pouch has gone dry. It doesn't become easier to absorb the grief. On the contrary, it grows more difficult.'

Despite his accomplishments in 2007 and, oblivious to the banner headlines he had commanded, Dario Franchitti was equally affected by the demise of McRae and his comrades. After all, it was less than a week from his IRL success before the news filtered through to the States that – on Saturday, September 15 – Colin, five-year-old Johnny, six-year-old Ben Porcelli and Graeme Duncan had died in the crash and, suddenly, everything else – the media interviews, the discussions over his future, a scheduled holiday – were placed on hold. 'That is the thing: as good as the rest of 2007 might have been to me, I will always regard it as the year we lost Colin and Johnny,' Franchitti told me. 'Colin was two things – he was a hero to people all over the world, to folk from countries who wouldn't have been able to find Lanarkshire on a map, but he was also my pal. We had done so many good things together, and it is terrible to think that he has been taken from us. It does make you realise what really matters in life.'

The next steps in Dario's carer would prove daunting and difficult, but he appreciated that racing glitches are like missed putts or botched penalty kicks – the only people who get steamed up about them are those who have a narrow perspective on this mortal coil. And as one admiring American journalist commented: 'The phrase "gentleman racer" can be derogatory, but when applied to Franchitti, it is a true compliment. In victory or defeat, he is a class act and he carries himself with style and panache. It's too bad that apparently he won't be sticking with the IndyCar series for an encore, because it seems pretty clear that our open-wheel racing is going to lose a hell of an ambassador.'

10

A NEW BEGINNING . . .

By the end of September, 2007, Dario Franchitti was ready to confirm what many in the motoring business already knew – that the thrill of the Indycars chase had dissipated and he was poised to embark on a fresh adventure in the helter-skelter, Dukes-of-Hazzard environment of NASCAR, which, for the uninitiated, stands for the National Association for Stock Car Auto Racing and is an activity as beloved of red-blooded Americans as shinty is to Highlanders in Scotland or Aussie Rules Football Down Under. It was a bold move on Dario's part, an opportunity at the age of 34 to enter a completely different version of racing, and attempt to learn the ropes quickly. But it was also a gamble, a surprisingly risky decision from somebody who had always been renowned for commonsense.

Yet there was certainly no disguising NASCAR's appeal, especially among Americans. Upon his entry, it was the second most popular professional sport in the United States, in terms of the all-important television ratings, ranking only behind the National Football League. The figures spoke for themselves: internationally, the races were broadcast in as many as 150 countries, it held 17 of the top 20 attended sporting events in the US, and boasted an estimated 75 million fans, who purchased more than $3bn of licensed products every year. In which circumstances, it has hardly surprising that somebody such as Franchitti, who had gained the major prizes in his Indy sphere, should be tempted by the chance of joining forces with the redoubtable Chip Ganassi, especially after being persuaded that he should take the plunge into the new world by his long-term rival, confidant and ally, Juan Pablo Montoya.

From Ganassi's perspective, the switch also represented an astute piece of business, or so it appeared when he and Dario formally announced the details of their multi-year deal on October 3. As if to heighten the sense of excitement, the news that the Scot was to link up with Chip Ganassi Racing and drive the No 40 Dodge vehicle in the 2008 Sprint Cup series was confirmed, in the course of a breathless press conference, where Franchitti's myriad achievements – 180 starts under his belt between CART and the IndyCar series, resulting in 18 wins, 17 poles, 63 top-five places and 95 top-10 spots – were emphasised. The media congregation was reminded, too, that he was about to become the first European driver in NASCAR's 59-year history to join the series on a full-time basis. It wasn't perhaps 'One small step for man' territory, but Ganassi had always prided himself on being his sport's equivalent of Don King: brash, in-your-face and hyperbolic.

All of which meant that it was no surprise when he rose to speak as if delivering the Sermon on the Mount and delivered the following message: 'Good morning, everybody. I guess I am announcing probably one of the worst-kept secrets in NASCAR over the last month or so, but it is still quite an honour and I am really happy to be sitting here this morning and that we have finally concluded the contract negotiations to free Dario to be here with us. I know he is looking forward to getting in the car, because he and I have been talking about this for a long, long time. I can probably tell that story now if you don't mind me telling the story [looks over to Dario]. You know, last year, he and I had some extensive talks about NASCAR and I said I would like him to drive for us, so let's do something. Then, I found myself in the unenviable position of having to call him up a few days later – he was going back to Scotland or something – and I had to call him up and tell him: "You know what, there is one guy on the planet who could have called and knocked you out of that seat [Montoya], and he and I have had a conversation and I gotta tell you that the seat is not available any more," declared Ganassi. 'But I also said to Dario: "Hey, you know, this [NASCAR] scene is a great place and I would like you to keep thinking about it, because you never know what will happen." And he went away and he did that. Things like that happen for a reason and all I could think about on the day of the Indianapolis 500 when Dario won the race, amid high drama, was that somehow it was meant to be. Then he won the IRL. I found myself in a no-lose situation, and that happened because he didn't come to NASCAR last year. Anyway, I am pretty excited to have him here and I am pretty excited to have him in our team. In fact, I am *really* excited. So without further ado, ladies and gentlemen, I give you Dario Franchitti.'

To his credit, Dario was as professional as ever, considering that his new owner had just told the audience he had been passed over for Montoya just a year previously. Yet I think it is important to convey, word for word, the tone of the Q and A session on that October day, if only to illustrate how rapidly matters can go downhill in sport. At the time, the mood was celebratory, the vibes relentlessly upbeat and positive: it was almost as if everybody had forgotten about the problems Montoya had suffered since joining the good ol' boys in the Southern states – he had even been booed by sections of the crowds on occasion, because he wasn't American – and his performances had been decidedly patchy. But now, all of a sudden, here was Franchitti being expected to transcend any difficulties and waltz into the NASCAR circuit as if it was the easiest thing in the world. It smacked of unreality, even as it was happening, and of fate setting him up.

But, of course, at the outset, positivity reigned. 'This is an absolute honour to be here today announcing that we are going to be driving for Chip and his team. I have had 11 great years in open-wheel racing, but the time came for a new challenge and this is it. It is going to be a heck of a challenge to learn everything. You know, just sitting here with the experience of zero, and I am going to be relying a lot on my new team-mates,' said Franchitti. 'I have already been quizzing Juan this morning about all of these different things. But when I get in the car in Talladega this weekend, with the ARCA car, it is going to be a big step. I am here to learn, first of all. As I mentioned, it is going to be a difficult, but an exciting challenge, and that is what I have been looking for.'

QUESTION: 'Dario, after you won Indy and what the season was like in July in Indy cars, you were complaining about not having enough time off at home. Do you have any idea that this [NASCAR] thing is pretty much a 12-month-a-year job?'

FRANCHITTI: 'I realise the schedule is going to be busy and I have been told to prepare for that. I spoke to Juan when Chip and I started talking. He [Chip] told me to call Juan and see what he thinks. So, Juan did the sales pitch. He said: "It is so much fun. You know the schedule, there are a lot of races, but it is so much fun. You are going to love it. You should really do it." But I know that it is going to be busy. I am here. I am here for the long term. I am here to learn first of all and to do the job that I am here to do.'

QUESTION: 'Here's something for Chip and for you, Dario. How will you prepare and what will you immediately start to do? What will you throw into the preparation?'

GANASSI: 'You know, obviously my relationship goes way back with Dario as well as with Juan. In 1999, Juan and Dario tied for the points and then we won on the tie-break. So, it goes back that far and probably further. Again, it is just racing. People always want to talk about how I am raiding the open-wheel series. But that is a bit of a slight to NASCAR. First of all, a lot of you have heard me say it. I don't care where the drivers come from. When good drivers are available, I think you have to look at them and take them. You have to use the best guys who are available out there. If a good guy becomes available, I think you are doing your team an injustice if you don't take a look at the situation. That's number one. Number two, I am not rating IndyCar racing or the IRL. Nobody is a bigger supporter of open-wheel racing and IndyCar racing than me and that series is continuing to grow. But you have to look at who are the best guys out there and if they are good drivers and they are available, then I want to talk to them.'

FRANCHITTI: 'I am just going to ask a lot of questions, first of all. The first time I sat in a stock car was yesterday, I got in the thing and had a seat fitted. I did a couple of years over in Germany with the DTM, so I have driven with a roof over my head before, but, as I said, it is all about learning and finding out new things. I am going to be around just asking Reed [Sorenson] and Juan, and all of the crew chiefs, and all the guys in the shop, and Chip. These guys have been through this before with Juan, so I think that is really a big help to me, because they went through those growing pains last season and just that transition has helped them gain a lot of knowledge. That is another major reason why I came to the team – because I knew in advance that this has all been done before.'

QUESTION: 'Did any of your wild rides [a reference to the two massive crashes, from which he emerged unscathed] from this past season lead you to this decision?'

FRANCHITTI: 'I would be lying if I said no. It was definitely a small part of the decision, but there was a lot more to it than that. I have been really intrigued by the challenge of NASCAR for quite a while now and that was the main reason. Winning the Indy 500 and the IRL championship made the decision even easier, because I had achieved what I wanted to achieve and it was time to move on and to jump into this world. My mind was already made up that I was leaving before the final race of the IRL season. That was just the icing on the cake from a terrific year and it felt really, really tremendous.'

QUESTION: 'What was your attraction [for joining NASCAR]? Was it the people, the sport, the racing, the basic fans, what was it that most appealed to you?

FRANCHITTI: 'It was the racing. I keep talking about new challenges. NASCAR intrigued me with the competitiveness of the series, and all the things that go into it, and as I said, the sales pitch that Mr Montoya carried out. I love the idea of learning something different, something which, at this point, I really have no clue about. I am going from being in a position of almost being a team leader to being just a rookie again, which is kind of interesting, but it is not as if we are going into this with our eyes shut.'

QUESTION: Dario, how hard do you think that this is going to be, realistically, apart from what Juan Montoya has told you? How do you plan to make friends in the garage?

FRANCHITTI: 'It's going to be tough. I am under no illusions here. This is probably the toughest challenge in my career and that is partly the reason I am doing it. It is going to be a very steep learning curve and I hope that I am up to the job. As far as making friends goes, I'm going to see the guys and talk to them. I know some of them a little bit, I am looking forward to meeting them, I have watched them on TV and have a lot of respect for them. Ashley turned to me and asked: "Now that you are doing this next year, do we have to watch it on television quite so much next year?"' [Laughter].

QUESTION: 'Were you disappointed last year when you got the phone call [from Ganassi] to say that Juan Montoya was going to be in that car, and also, do you feel that when people such as yourself are leaving the IRL, it is hurting the sport?'

FRANCHITTI: 'As far as leaving the IRL goes, I think the series is much bigger than any one driver and that there are a lot of young guys coming up to take my place and they still have a load of great drivers, so I don't think that my departure will hurt it. As far as was I disappointed [over losing out to Montoya], yeah I was, I was disappointed by that. But I am really glad that things turned out the way they have this year. Looking back now, with hindsight, I would have hated to have left open-wheel racing and the Andretti Green Racing team at the end of 2006, because it was such a disastrous year for us. So I am much happier to be leaving with the record that we have established in 2007.'

The words were to prove prescient. NASCAR *was* every bit as treacherous and testing as anybody could have feared, and there were no short, sharp routes to success for Franchitti any more than there had been for Montoya. On the contrary, once the stage-managed conference chat had subsided and the American media had carried a series of glowing profiles about the new kid on the stock-car block – which invariably seemed to be accompanied by photographs of Ashley Judd – Dario's initial experiences on Ganassi's behalf served to confirm his fears that what he knew about life in the Busch car or, even more dauntingly, the COT (Car of Tomorrow) could have been inserted on the back of a postcard. It was as if his life had flipped back to 1995 when he was learning his trade in the DTM, and his early performances offered an illustration of the task he faced in straddling the divide between the two diverse forms of motor sport. His maiden race in a stock car, at Talladega Superspeedway on October 5, saw him finish 17th. Then he launched his NASCAR campaign with a 33rd-place Craftsman Truck Series showing at the Martinsville Speedway and followed that up by coming in 32nd in Memphis on October 27. It was perhaps premature to write him off on this flimsy evidence, but there were already snipers lurking, amidst the Busches, waiting for him to fall flat on his face. It was a chastened Franchitti who assessed his initial displays at Hallowe'en.

'I never pretended that this was going to be easy and there is an incredible amount to learn, but we knew what a challenge this was and we have been justified in thinking that. Driving the Busch car has come easier than driving the COT. I have tested the latter at Atlanta in a group session yesterday and Monday and I found that very, very difficult, so I know I've still got a long way to go in that regard. As for the Busch car, I've been getting into that and finding my feet. The result wasn't very good in Memphis, but we qualified in third and were running right up front all day until we had a brake problem and that set us back. So, that was something positive. I think the COT is going to take a bit longer to get comfortable in, because it is so different from anything I have ever driven in the past. With the big, high centre of gravity, there is just no grip with the thing, so I felt I was kind of thrown in at the deep end in Atlanta, having never driven a Cup car of any kind. And that experience showed me how far I have still got to progress.

'But as for comparing an Indy car and a stock car on this track [the Kentucky Speedway], it is completely different. There are completely different lines. With IndyCar, we are probably using a third of the track. In NASCAR, we are using every inch of it. The Indy vehicle is a lot faster, but the impression in the stock car is equally as good, because when you are on the limit of the performance of the car, anything feels quick. Overall, what can I say at this stage? It is interesting to have to deal with the changes – the tyres wear, the balance of the car changes and the weather dictates the balance of the car and its performance. So it is all very different from what I have been used to.'

At this juncture, the Ganassi organisation remained defiantly optimistic. Time, or so they reckoned, was on their side, because the serious NASCAR business would not commence until 2008 and Franchitti was pencilled in for a significant amount of cramming up on his homework in the intervening period. That test on Hallowe'en had been designed to provide Dario with a contrasting set of experiences behind the wheel, and, according to the CGR Busch Series program manager, Brian Pattie, he was satisfied with his new charge's responses to what had been a stern induction. 'We set up a schedule trying to get him a lot of laps in different cars at different facilities which he hadn't seen before. Memphis was one, Martinsville another and obviously Talladega,' said Pattie. 'The main challenge is to understand the way he delivers information. In the past, Dario has always had engineering and the telemetry telling the guys [in the garage] what was happening with the car, before he told them. But NASCAR is highly regulated and telemetry is only allowed during tests, so we are doing our best to give him the feedback, telemetry-wise versus what he is feeling. Even if we change something and we know it's wrong, we want to show what it's like. That is our biggest objective and, overall, Dario has scored high marks. The more laps he runs, the better he gets, which has to be encouraging.'

Even as he was grappling with the intricacies of this unfamiliar regime, Ashley spelled out what she thought of her husband's decision. 'It is difficult to overstate how proud I am of him,' she wrote. 'His willingness to chuck everything he knew – and at which he excelled at the highest level – for something totally new and unknown, makes me think he is utterly courageous. How many of us have that humility and adventurous spirit?' Similar sentiments were echoed by the likes of Sir Jackie Stewart and Allan McNish, who stated their mutual opinion that Dario was exactly the sort of restless, redoubtable character who would seize his NASCAR opportunity and circumnavigate any obstacles placed in his path, even though both anticipated that any substantial advance would take months, not weeks, and that it might be 2009 before he was pushing for Sprint Cup glory. In short, the majority of observers were careful and cautious, unwilling to predict that his move would be anything other than a marathon, not a sprint. But what nobody could have forecast was how the impact of the credit crunch on both sides of the Atlantic would result in belt-tightening, cost-cutting and fiscal pruning in an industry which had hitherto been renowned as a licence to print money. Essentially, Franchitti, and his compatriots, Stewart and McNish, may have imagined that Ganassi had entered into partnership for the long haul. But as the Gershwins wrote: 'It Ain't Necessarily So.'

That, however, was in the future. As of November and December 2007, Dario's star was firmly in the ascendant and when we spoke shortly before Christmas, he was as buoyant and exuberant as ever, while casting his gaze over the coruscating stream of events which had thrust him into the spotlight. 'The only downside when I won the IRL competition was that, because I had already agreed the NASCAR deal, I didn't have the luxury of sitting back and being able to enjoy my success. But what an incredible season it had been for me and what a roller-coaster of emotions there have been. Finishing in the lead at the Indy 500 when the rain intervened summed up how things went in my favour as the summer passed and it was the same when Scott Dixon's car ground to a halt on the last corner of the title-deciding race. In previous years, there had been little blips, strokes of misfortune, weekends where things didn't go according to plan, but I definitely couldn't have asked for better fortune this time around. I mean, to walk away from two serious accidents with barely a scratch on me was remarkable, but after everything I had been through in 2006, and stretching back to 1999, maybe we got payback.

'That doesn't alter the fact I am entering a new chapter in my life by going to NASCAR, and it is a huge transition. Until now, throughout my career, I have only had to deal with minor variations when I have changed from one circuit to another, but now I am in a stock car, which is heavier than a single-seater vehicle, it handles in a different way from anything I have ever been used to before, and so I am not setting myself any goals at this stage. However, as you might expect, I am striving to be competitive. As ever.'

In the weeks since September, Franchitti's achievements had been properly rewarded by his peers, precipitating a series of transatlantic sojourns to collect assorted honours. He was the Sports Personality of the Year at the Scottish Sports Awards in Glasgow early in December and was presented with the Gregor Grant Award in London a few days later, in addition to gaining the prestigious Stewart Medal, the John Romanes Swift Trophy and other symbols of recognition from the British Racing Drivers' Club, as well as being nominated in the United States as one of their 'Speed Performers of the Year'.

Yet it was a measure of his character that he remained free of the selfishness and egotism which tended to pervade those in the fast lane. 'I try to keep tabs on as many different things as possible and it has obviously been a good year for Scottish football, both for the national side and with three clubs [Celtic, Rangers and Aberdeen] advancing in Europe,' Franchitti told me, prior to being glued to the screen for the Parkhead side's Champion's League joust with mighty Barcelona. 'Quite apart from me, we should all be very proud of Scotland's continuing success in motor-sport, because my brother, Marino, did very well in the US Le Mans series, Allan McNish has just completed a terrific season, and Paul Di Resta performed really creditably in the DTM Championship, and I have great hopes for the lad. Basically, if the guys at Mercedes look after him – which they will – Paul is a fantastic talent and, in my opinion, he is as good as anybody I have ever seen racing at his age [he was then 21]. So there are plenty of reasons why we can be cheerful about the future, but, for now, my priority has to be succeeding in NASCAR.'

The silverware and plaudits were welcome, but on either side of the Yuletide, Franchitti discovered the full extent of the challenge confronting him. He had appreciated soon enough that he could tear up the IRL driving manual, because it was immaterial on the NASCAR circuit, but even Dario seemed surprised by the scale of the metamorphosis and, despite acquiring snippets of information here, nuggets of valuable advice there, he had to return to the basics which had marked his introduction to motor-sport in the first place.

This led to him seeking counsel with his Ganassi colleagues, Juan Montoya, Reed Sorenson and David Stremme, and he also maintained contact with his former AGR allies, Tony Kanaan, Marco Andretti and Danica Patrick, but despite the assistance and succour which they passed on to one another, he recognised there was no substitute for racing experience and something of a Catch-22 situation gradually developed. On the one hand, Dario needed laps, and lots of them, and had to test himself at the highest level, which meant pursuing rides in the Sprint Cup. But, on the other, the more he sought to engineer a breakthrough, the greater his lack of NASCAR knowledge became evident. The problem was exacerbated by a rather strange scenario, where Franchitti weaved in and out of the main competition and the second-tier Nationwide Series without being allowed to crank up momentum in either event. At the outset, he wasn't overly worried, but he was on serious money with Ganassi – reported to be in the region of between $20m and $30m over three years – and, understandably, there was only so long that a hard-nosed capitalist organisation would tolerate its drivers flailing around. And although it was also true that he was by no means the sole debutant making his graduation into the stock-car sphere – the others comprised the former Formula One and Indy 500 champion, Jacques Villeneuve, the ex-Champ Car winner, Patrick Carpentier, and the three-time Indy Racing League victor, Sam Hornish, Jnr – Franchitti was the outsider, the only European in the pack. Considering how NASCAR had long been perceived as a bastion of Deep South (white) American values, he privately acknowledged that there would be a greater amount of focus on him than the rest.

'I used to watch these races a lot – and I really mean a lot – and I thought it would be a challenge to drive one of those cars. I had heard how demanding it was, but little did I know how big a challenge it would be. Sometimes you have to be careful what you wish for,' said Franchitti, following a test at Homestead in Florida, as the prelude to appearing in the Ford 300, where he qualified in 20th, but his event ended abruptly with a crash on the 44th lap. 'So far, I have been getting used to the car set-ups and learning how to drive and race these cars and I am seeing progress, which is cool. Juan and David and Reed have been very helpful, and so has Jimmie Johnson [a stalwart of the NASCAR milieu], who has told me to come to him at any time, which I have been doing on a regular basis. But you can't hurry these things. Tony [Kanaan] called me from Japan a few days ago. He is driving a formula racing car there and he is having difficulty in adapting to it, and we both laughed at the fact that we had gotten involved in situations which were giving us difficulties. But, on a serious note, this is a big deal for me and I want to make a success of this, because I have managed to do that wherever else I have raced in my career.'

As 2007 morphed into 2008 – Dario and Ashley spent the festive period at their palatial residence in Tennessee – Franchitti was able to enjoy the start to the new year by gaining a first glimpse of his image on the fabled Borg-Warner Trophy (awarded to the Indy 500 champion) and walking away with the coveted Jerry Titus prize at a star-studded ceremony in Indianapolis on January 12. In the midst of his travails with the NASCAR vehicles, this was an evening where he could unwind and relax, however briefly, and he was in particularly loquacious form during the banquet at the Hyatt-Regency Hotel, swapping banter with some of the most revered names in the United States motoring firmament and lapping up the anecdotes and recollections of the NASCAR Cup series champion, Jimmy Johnson, the Champ Car World Series' Sebastien Bourdais, and other luminaries such as Tony Schumacher, Jeff Gordon and Mika Salo.

Indeed, on a night when his best qualities shone through,

Dario said that his only regret was the fact that he would not be able to defend his Indy 500 crown in May, given the scheduling clashes between the event and his NASCAR commitments, which correctly had to take priority. 'The timing is impossible, and at the same time, you can't come back here and be competitive in a one-off deal because the competition is too tough, but you have to believe that winning this prize [he pointed to the Borg-Warner trophy] is one of the greatest things which has ever happened to me. I tried so hard to win the race, and it is such a long race that so many things can go wrong, but it was fantastic to make the breakthrough and, to be honest, I was in shock for about a week afterwards.'

He was in his element in this environment. The attendant throng were all genuine motoring aficionados, who had devoted years of service to their passion, and time-wasters needed not apply. Dario also used these first few weeks in January to reacquaint himself with some of his best friends as Chip Ganassi assembled a luminous line-up for the 46th Rolex 24 at the Daytona International Speedway, where Franchitti was installed in the same team as Juan Pablo Montoya, Scott Pruett and Memo Rojas. The quartet warmed up for this endurance test by posting excellent pre-race times, which illustrated their cumulative ability when placed in the correct type of vehicle. However, in contrast, Dario continued to react to the NASCAR puzzle as if tackling one of Araucaria's thornier *Guardian* crosswords and although there were still noises from the Ganassi camp, which equated to the show-business maxim: 'It will be all right on the night', the pressure was growing within the Dodge camp as an arduous season grew closer.

Thankfully, what *was* all right was the commanding manner in which Franchitti and his colleagues powered their Lexus Victory to a convincing triumph in the Rolex event.

The Ganassi ensemble, who slipped into their roles with the practised harmony of The Manhattan Transfer, enjoyed a virtually trouble-free race, dominating most of their rivals from start to finish, and led for 252 of the 695 laps, ending up comfortably in front of the Pontiac Riley team of Alex Gurney, Jon Fogarty, Jimmie Johnson and Jimmy Vasser. Their showing was doubly impressive, because heavy rain was the catalyst for treacherous conditions, with no fewer than 24 caution periods being required. This amounted to more than six hours of yellow flag conditions, where the participants had to be at their sharpest and eagle-eyed, and where they all had to slot into their respective roles, otherwise the whole campaign would have fallen apart.

'That was tough, and we were up against a lot of really hard, fast cars out there,' said Pruett, who was toasting his third success in the Rolex 24. 'Everybody did a great job, You always had to push hard in the car, and it was pretty difficult for long stretches, because it was wet, then it was dry, and then it was a little bit of wet and then you weren't really sure whether to go with the wet or dry tyres. And then it rained again!

'That always makes for a really tough race and I think that is why we saw so many cautions. These kind of conditions are really horrible to drive in, and, in my view, this is the most difficult 24-hour race in the world. [This is a view which will be hotly disputed by someone such as Allan McNish, a two-time victor in the original Le Mans marathon]. It's a true test of man, machine and team, because you can't appreciate all the effort which has gone into getting the car right before you even show up at the track.'

Franchitti was rather more circumspect, but had clearly relished the opportunity to renew his acquaintance with a mixture of former and current colleagues and adversaries. 'It's a really good way to start 2008 and the cars were prepared perfectly. I thought that my job was to get through my stints and stay on the pace and not push any dents in the car or crash the car. And it makes it more difficult that every time I got in the car, it started to rain! It was a hell of a team effort and it means a lot to win this race,' said Dario, who sped towards the podium as if it was his maiden appearance on a prize-giving plinth. 'We all worked very hard and we did what we had to do, because you can't win something like this without everybody pulling their weight and heading in the right direction.'

Normally, January is a grim month, a time for wrapping up, keeping the home fires burning, dreading the arrival of the monthly credit-card bills, dodging any viruses, and wishing the darkness and gloom would relent if only ever so slightly. Yet Franchitti's disposition in Daytona was as sunny as the elements were saturnine. Regrettably, as far as 2008 was concerned, it was a mirror image which would continue into the summer.

11

. . . And A Sharp Exit?

NASCAR has always been a law unto itself, operating by its own rules and regulations, and unconcerned with what the rest of the world might think of the slightly loopy manner in which its participants have transformed the animated mayhem of 'Wacky Races' into real-life flesh and blood, without ever quite erasing the impression there is something unreal about the whole enterprise. When Dario Franchitti announced in October, 2007, that he was linking up with Chip Ganassi and Felix Sabates, in a No 40 Dodge Charger vehicle, it sounded as if Will Ferrell and Steve Carell might be lurking in the wings, waiting to unearth a comedy sketch from the school of *Saturday Night Live.*'

But no, the story was serious, it was a multi-million-dollar deal and therefore to be treated with the reverence and solemnity which typifies the general American attitude to sports reporting. In the interim, between October and February, 2008, I e-mailed four Stateside motoring journalists, and asked them whether they believed Dario would make a successful transition from open-wheel vehicles to the stock-car circuit. Their responses were, from a British perspective at least, rather incredible. One actually replied – in, believe it or not, an e-mail – 'No comment', another said he felt uncomfortable discussing the future of any sports personality publicly and the other two requested anonymity, which rather screwed up the point of the venture. And yet, and yet, there was perhaps a touch of method to their reticence, on the evidence of how touchy NASCAR enthusiasts appear to be whenever anybody dares to suggest that their beloved sport may not represent the apotheosis of human endeavour. In some respects, it was reminiscent of the time when I spent a week aboard a cruise ship, the *Ocean Princess*, which was travelling between Vancouver and Anchorage in Alaska in 2000, and whose crew decided to organise an urgent lifeboat drill almost as soon we had set sail. Amidst the chaos, a septuagenarian woman next to me was quizzed by an incredibly patient female steward: 'And where is your husband?' To which, she replied once, twice, thrice, as though the answer would be of any use whatsoever in a genuine emergency: 'Oh, he's in the john. But he won't be there much longer.' Later, on the same afternoon, the first mate participated in a meet-and-greet session and asked the passengers where we all came from. His inquiry: 'How many of you are Americans?' was greeted with loud whoops and the raising of a majority of hands. The Canadian contingent were more reserved in their reply, but still formed a significant number of the manifest. A hundred or so of us indicated that we were from the United Kingdom, a similar number followed suit from France, Germany, Italy and Japan, and eventually, nearly everybody had been accounted for, apart from a vociferous band of brethren, who were beginning to grow restless, hungry and thirsty in the corner and vented their displeasure at being kept waiting before getting to the buffet. Eventually, our greeter turned to them and asked: 'So where do all you gentlemen come from?' 'Texas', responded one of the loudest and paunchiest of the group.

'But that is part of America,' declared the by-now harassed naval employee, at which point three or four voices piped up in unison: 'Not for as long as we are still able to draw breath, it isn't!'

That answer resonates in my mind, because it embodies many of the characteristics of NASCAR: a combination of insularity, bravado, unintentional humour and decibels, decibels and more decibels. One of my e-mail respondents finally agreed to offer a comment on Franchitti and his switch to stock cars, and it shed a significant amount of light on why so few non-Americans enjoy success in this bear-pit. 'To be honest, it's always going to be tough for an "outsider" to make the grade in NASCAR, because it remains very "provincial",' wrote my source, a respected West Coast-based journalist. 'That is not necessarily a criticism, just the reality of the situation. There is no doubt about Dario's ability. The only question is whether his team has what it takes to give him winning equipment. This might apply in most forms of sport, but is particularly true in NASCAR, where it appears that drivers have to "pay their dues" before they are likely to earn real success.' Reading between the lines, this hinted at the parochialism which surrounds so much of US sport – the World Series, anyone! – and my other (anonymous) correspondent was even more scathing in his suggestion that stock-car racing was beyond parody, which maybe explained why Ferrell's supposed comedy, *Talladega Nights*, was about as funny as colonic irrigation. 'Dario has taken a huge gamble here, because although he is being paid plenty of money, I would have thought it was very unlikely that he would break into the NASCAR ranks at the age of 34 or 35 after driving in different types of motor-sport for so long. What he should have done was stay in the Indy Racing League, or join his brother, Marino, in the American Le Mans Series. But for him to become a success in NASCAR, a lot of the guys who want to root for their own people and hate the idea of foreigners taking Americans' jobs are going to have to broaden their minds. And, privately, with a lot of these folks, that is a contradiction in terms.'

Some of this was doubtless unfair, but even from the outset, NASCAR and sophistication have gone together like George W Bush and oratory. The association was founded by William France Jnr, on February 21, 1948, and the original points system was written on a bar-room napkin. The first commissioner of the sport was Erwin 'Cannonball' Baker, who would demonstrate a car's worth by driving it from New York to Los Angeles, earned the sobriquet 'King of the Road', and whose feats were posthumously recognised in the Hollywood movie *The Cannonball Run*. In the early 1950s, according to the official records, 'The United States Navy stationed Bill France Jnr at the Moffett Federal Airfield in northern California and his father asked him to look up Bob Barkhimer in San Jose. Barkhimer was a star of midget car racing from the World War Two era and subsequently ran 22 different speedways as the head of the California Stock Car Racing Association', becoming one of the most prominent people in the business (and gaining the nickname 'Barky'), alongside the France family and the Cannonball kid. In some respects, this might be seen as relatively down-to-earth and healthy, but there remains something curious and arcane, not to say impenetrable, about the manner in which NASCAR has gripped and captivated so many fans.

However, as Dario approached the Daytona 500 in February, 2008, the questions hanging in the air were: 'Will he make the grade?' and 'Will he be accepted into the fold?'

Certainly, he did not lack for any mod cons, after being supplied with a million-dollar motor home, which included state-of-the-art technology, a projection television and a DVD collection which was the envy of most Tinseltown producers

– hardly surprising, given that Ashley was a member of the Academy of Motion Picture Arts and Sciences. But although the couple generated a significant buzz, it was interesting how much of the coverage centred on the wife and not the man who was poised to do the driving. '"We have not had anybody of Ashley Judd's stature here on a regular basis before," said Lowe's Motor Speedway president, H A "Humpy" Wheeler, a veteran of more than 40 years in NASCAR,' reported *USA* Today. '"And it is not going to take him any longer to have success than Montoya. People love our celebrities and they help make our sport bigger and better. It's the publicity you get that you don't expect."' The same newspaper also quoted Monica Pickerill, a 56-year-old from Lebanon, Kentucky, who co-owned a Dodge dealership with her husband and was gushing about Judd. 'She's the new superstar of the pits. Women embrace her. Everyone identifies with her.' This might have been appropriate if Ashley had been a new Danica Patrick or Sarah Fisher, a female with the qualities to thrive at the highest level of motor sport, but it was positively bizarre that so much fuss was focused on her *watching* Dario, standing by her man.

All the same, Franchitti's testing displays and early outings for Ganassi had been underwhelming and the trend continued at Daytona. The defending champion, Kevin Harvick, had ruffled feathers with his contention that the influx of rookies to NASCAR was happening too quickly in a bid to address falling viewing figures, but he may have been justified in his assertion that the former open-wheel drivers were 'going down the wrong road by not starting their careers in a lower-tier stock car series and would find the Sprint Cup racing harder than any of them imagined'. It was difficult to disagree when Montoya and Franchitti finished 32nd and 33rd respectively in Florida, the duo sufficiently off the pace that all the attention rightly focused on the winner, Ryan Newman, and the battle of the Busches, Kurt and Kyle, who ended second and fourth respectively.

There then ensued what was to develop into a depressingly repetitive strain syndrome: the unaccustomed sound of Dario fretting over consistently poor performances. 'We finished – that is about all I can say right now. The guys gave it their absolute best shot and we had great pit stops all day long,' he said in the aftermath. 'The car was a little slow, but the main problem was that anytime anybody got behind me, and I was in the middle of the pack, the car was unbelievably loose. I had to run at the back or I was going to crash, so I need to work to give the guys better information to set the car up.'

Nobody should have imagined he would soar to instant victories in the NASCAR arena. After all, in the previous season, Montoya had triumphed once at Sonoma, but had posted only six top-ten finishes in more than 30 races and had been struggling in the latter half of the season, despite gaining the accolade of rookie of the year. Yet, whether it was the excessive burden of expectations which had been heaped on his shoulders or the fact that Ashley had other commitments – such as her livelihood in the film industry – the early euphoria which had heralded Dario's arrival in NASCAR became a slow puncture.

Statistics can be as dry as dust. They can also be misleading. And it would be a waste of time to detail the minutiae of every glitch which afflicted and bedevilled the hapless Scot as the weeks elapsed and he toiled for signs of improvement. On March 10, he raced the Fastenal Dodge No 40 not once, but twice, at the Atlanta Motor Speedway, recording a 28th-place result in the Nationwide Series on the Saturday and then, 24 hours later, slipping to 33rd – again – in the frontline NASCAR series, although he was battling a flu bug in the second event. On the surface, these were hardly disasters, and Franchitti had secured an early lead in the rookie class over his team-mate, Bryan Clauson, in the NNS, and a two-point advantage over Sam Hornish Jnr in the Sprint Cup. Yet, behind the scenes, Ganassi was having problems in a contracting market place securing the requisite finance to maintain Dario's car. The harder the team worked, the more they stood still.

'It's the same every week for us, a big learning experience. I cannot believe how loose the cars were all day, but I think everybody was in the same boat. We were just hanging on. We hit the wall a couple of times just on exit, with the thing being so loose and the rear being toed-out,' said Franchitti, with as much enthusiasm as he could muster, given his sickness and shivers in the snowy Atlanta setting. 'I drove as hard as I could all day and my guys did a terrific job with the pit stops. But we just couldn't get the adjustments in the car to handle the way we needed ... as I've said repeatedly, it is important to get experience. But it would be nice to have some better results to show for it.'

If there was any consolation, it lay in the sight of Hornish Jnr similarly labouring to make the transition, although, to his credit, Franchitti has never been somebody to indulge in schadenfreude. On the contrary, as the pair reached the end of March, still beset by gremlins, and arrived in Richmond, Virginia, under increasing pressure to improve their displays, they compared notes and privately agreed that NASCAR was a much tougher environment than they had originally envisaged. Both men had triumphed at this venue in the past, steering their open-wheel cars to success on the lightning-quick oval, but somehow, that knowledge offered scant relief for the beleaguered duo. 'When you show up at a circuit where you have won before, you think to yourself: "Okay, I know this place, so I can go out and do a good job",' said Franchitti, following the opening day of tests, where he was 24th fastest. 'But one of the things I am learning is that it is actually easier for me to go to a track where I have never performed before, because then I have no pre-conceived ideas about what I am doing. Basically, you have to learn on the job and the whole [NASCAR] thing has been much harder than I thought it would be. You are racing against the best in the business and then you throw in a couple of mechanical issues which have cost us and you can understand why we have had problems.'

Hornish, for his part, had competed in the Nationwide Series in 2007 and felt that this had provided him with a slight edge over his fellow Indy 500 champion. 'I have had my eyes opened to some things that were very different from where we were in IndyCars. The way I look at it, we have a tremendous opportunity to do better than we have done. Our team is new and it is like putting together a puzzle. We have a new driver, a new crew chief, and a new team, but while we are trying very hard, we still don't know whether all of the pieces will fit. The bottom line is that 2008 is a building year for us.'

The couple had employed different phraseology, but the underlying message was strikingly similar. Yet, regardless of the graft, the lashings of perspiration and commitment from the 70 people who were part of Franchitti's team, weekends came and went without any noticeable improvement and, on occasion, the situation worsened. He failed to qualify for the NASCAR event at the Texas Motor Speedway at the beginning of April and that prompted a stinging broadside from Ganassi, who, for the first time, publicly questioned whether his three cars were working for the common good. 'Frankly, there are 46 cars out there and if you can't beat three of them, it is pretty pathetic. I certainly have all the faith in the world in his [Franchitti's] driving abilities. I don't think it is that. The fact of the matter is that we didn't give him a car he was capable of doing anything with,' fumed a Chip not so much hot as boiling. He seemed sceptical as to whether his separate crews were actively interested in creating a solid foundation for success. 'We're not working as a team. You can't have guys who are fast and guys that are slow, it doesn't make any sense. These guys [Franchitti, Montoya and Sorenson], these teams, are not talking to one another, they are not working together and they are not using all the resources which are available to them. That is how you end up in a fix like the one we are in. This is a tough sport, it's a tough damn business and we really are better than we have shown so far this season. We know the issues, we know how to make cars go fast and, for some reason, we just aren't doing it. This goes back to people and procedures and policies that people are going to have to adopt. People just can't keep doing it the old-school way. If I need to make personnel changes, I won't hesitate.'

These words left no room for misinterpretation, but there was no escape from the slough of despond. At the Phoenix International Raceway in Arizona in the middle of April, there were signs of a genuine breakthrough when Franchitti ran towards the summit of the speed chart for most of the NASCAR Nationwide Series, and eventually qualified for the 312-lap Sprint Cup event in 21st place – a career best for the Scot. But although he was competitive for most of the proceedings, he got tripped up, following an unfortunate yellow, and could only manage 32nd, which was nothing like the sort of progress he was pursuing. 'Sometimes you get lucky and sometimes you're unlucky and we were unlucky tonight. We came to the pit road about three laps before the yellow came out and that put us an extra lap down, so that was that. We were two laps down, instead of just one, and despite running top-15 times pretty much all night, we didn't get what we deserved,' said Franchitti. 'I am really proud of the team, and the job they have done this week coming back from previous disappointments, and the way they worked in qualifying. If we keep doing this, we'll be going forward and we are closer to the top 35 than we were going into the race. [They were in 39th place]. I think that we can qualify at Talladega and we will just keep on pushing . . .' But there is probably no need to continue because you have heard it all before. In his defence, Dario was being remarkably loyal, refusing to blame others for his woes, and living up to his reputation as a consummate team player, with no interest in narcissism or ego. But if something could go wrong, it was going wrong.

And then, as if some diabolical puppeteer was intent on wreaking fresh havoc, a terse statement was issued by his employers on April 26, which read: 'Chip Ganassi Racing with Felix Sabates (CGRFS) driver Dario Franchitti will not compete in the NASCAR Sprint Cup Series race on Sunday at Talladega Superspeedway after suffering a slight fracture in his left ankle as a result of a collision on lap 11 in Saturday's NASCAR Nationwide Series (NNS) event. Franchitti will be re-evaluated early next week, but arrangements are underway to find a substitute driver to pilot the No 40 Dodge car in tomorrow's race at Talladega.' The announcement bore the signs of an organisation which was running out of patience with its newcomer, but Franchitti was entitled to wonder why the fates were conspiring against him. His injury had occurred when his vehicle had blown a tyre – the sort of innocuous, everyday incident which can be annoying, but not career-threatening, and definitely nowhere in the same category as the brace of crashes from which he had walked away unhurt in the Indy Racing League. But now, there was the opposite of momentum in his life. There was stasis, and his task in turning things around made Sisyphus's job appear a piece of cake by comparison.

Worst of all, for somebody with Franchitti's independent nature, events were spiralling out of his control. It wasn't simply that he ended up spending a month out of commission, but his rivals had settled into a groove: the likes of Hornish Jnr had advanced while Dario was incapacitated, and there was still no sign that Ganassi had discovered any long-term investment for the No 40 Dodge, without which he was pouring cash into a black hole. Even when Franchitti returned on June 1 at the Dover International Speedway, in the NNS on the notorious Monster Mile, with a creditable 15th place, there was the scent of trouble in the air and although he remained as equitable and articulate as ever, the season which had promised so much was stalled in third or fourth gear. 'My ankle is fine and I can put weight on it, but we didn't want to do too much too quickly and risk further damage,' said Franchitti. 'We tested [this week] at Pocono raceway and everything seemed to be working well. But it has been a long four weeks and it feels really good to be back in the car.' 'It is tough when you have been out of the car for that length of time. I was able to work out to some extent in the gym, but I wasn't able to run, so that has been tough. We found out that the steering wheel was a little bit big, so I was struggling to get my arm up enough sometimes. It was definitely the toughest race I have done so far, but my first experience at Dover was quite something and now we can move ahead.'

During his enforced break, Dario had watched his former rival, Scott Dixon, triumph in the Indy 500 at the Brickyard. He had also relished Danica Patrick's historic victory in the IRL in Japan and wouldn't have been human if he hadn't reflected on whether he would have been better staying in his old domain. But he refused to be drawn on the issue or wallow in self-pity. 'I love the Indy 500, it's a fabulous race. But I have closed that door and I am happy with the choice I made. I was fortunate to leave the Indy scene on top and it is nice to have this new challenge in NASCAR. I am settled in.'

Perhaps he believed this. But within a month, Ganassi had shut his team down.

The last straw arrived at Sonoma in California in late June. This was a place where Franchitti had led for more laps – at the Infineon Raceway – than any other driver in Indycar history and had gained the second-biggest amount of money in the open-wheel realm at the track. In short, he knew the circuit as well as the back of his hand and yet looked like a stranger in a strange land in failing to qualify for another race, after finishing a dismal 45th out of 47 competitors. Suddenly, there was a dearth of sympathy for his plight and one leading NASCAR source was scathing over Dario's display. 'Nothing that happened in the past mattered on Friday, when Franchitti looked as if he had never been on the race track before,' wrote David Caraviello. 'He stalled out and needed to be pushed by a wrecker. He hopped a curb and rumbled through the dirt in practice. And then he lumbered through one of the slowest qualifying attempts of the 47 drivers, who were vying for a spot in a Toyota 350, a lap which bettered only those posted by David Reutimann and West Coast touring driver, Brandon Ash.'

Franchitti admitted: 'We were just loose, very, very loose, and that was it. The other guys complained about it a bit, but I think we were maybe even looser than them. We felt we got caught out with it and I am shocked that we came to a road course and didn't qualify.' Franchitti was using terms which had grown depressingly familiar. But there was no longer any disguising his paucity of performance in a brutal pursuit. He had now missed five races with his ankle injury, failed to qualify for a couple of events, and had not finished better than 22nd in the nine Sprint Cup starts which he had made since the season premiere. Although he claimed that he felt he was more competitive in June than in January, he had been involved in an accident at Pocono and limped home in 41st. At Michigan, his vehicle had given up the ghost and he had been listed last. And now, here was the nadir at Sonoma. 'It has definitely been much harder than I thought, but I can see things moving forward. If you are the type to give up easily, this isn't the place to be, but I am not about to give it up and I know that the guys in my team aren't either, so we will just keep going.'

This dogged perseverance was admirable, but it couldn't mask the sense of disappointment which had filtered through the entire Ganassi NASCAR operation. It was therefore no huge surprise when the owner mulled over his options, in the aftermath of the Infineon fiasco. According to insiders, he struggled to sleep on it for the best part of a week, and was clearly wrestling between his heart and his head. But in business circles, the latter usually prevails and so it transpired that on July 1, Ganassi publicly announced he was shutting down Dario's race team, with immediate effect, because of a lack of sponsorship. It was a crushing blow to the staff involved in the No 40 Dodge organisation, but with Franchitti languishing in 41st position in the NASCAR standings, nobody could claim to be unduly surprised. None of this eased the pain and misery which was inevitably felt by the 70 employees who lost their jobs, as a consequence of Ganassi's failure to track down sustained investment for his third NASCAR team, but the reality was that many sponsors' wallets has snapped shut as the American economy slipped into recession – long-term backers, Coors Light, had withdrawn their support at the end of the previous season and even the marketable Franchitti had not attracted any company, willing to be associated on a year-by-year, rather than a week-to-week basis, with one of the most bankable driving stars in the United States.

And, whatever words might have been used to describe Ganassi, he was never likely to be described as a sentimentalist. 'There is no money and it makes no sense to be running this out of my own pocket, so I had to put a stop to it,' said the entrepreneur, who sparked a degree of surprise by electing to continue bankrolling Reed Sorenson, who was lying only 31st in the NASCAR ranks. 'This is a difficult decision which did not come without its share of anguish. But, in an increasingly tough business environment, continuing to run a car without proper funding has become a lot harder. If I had kept it going, I ran the risk of dragging the other two cars down and I didn't want that.'

The downbeat nature of the announcement was in stark contrast to the fanfares which had signalled Franchitti's move to NASCAR, and within nine months, a fraught birthing process had been rendered stillborn. Dario had discovered in the worst possible circumstances that success in one branch of the motoring sector is never any guarantee of plaudits or viable results in another, but it was characteristic of the man that he was initially less concerned with his own worries than the problems of those employees who had worked unstintingly for him, in what had ultimately proved a futile pursuit. 'This is about a lot more people than just me and there is a whole bigger picture to consider. In fact, I think that is something which has given me some perspective on the whole issue,' he said, in response to Ganassi's actions. 'It wasn't just people directly connected to the Dodge 40 car, it was people from the front office, from all different departments, and I feel bad for them, every single one of them. This is the first time in my career that such a thing has happened and it is not a good feeling.

'If the money is not there, the money is not there, and

I can understand Chip's position, but it was very frustrating, because I really felt that we were getting on top of things and finding our way, which is one of the reasons why I certainly have no intention of walking away from NASCAR if I can help it. Sure, there were some very difficult days, but there were also days where we felt that we were making progress and these days were a lot of fun. So I would love to start again with the level of experience that I have in NASCAR now, rather than where I was at the start of 2008. I got the feeling that this year, whatever could go wrong did go wrong, but I think that we were turning things around.'

In the days ahead, Franchitti held talks with Ganassi and reinforced his determination to carry on his learning process, even if it meant being pitched in and out of the Nationwide Series. At 35, there were some observers who mentioned the possibility that he might slip quietly into retirement – and it seemed poignant that only 24 hours before his NASCAR team was closed down, his compatriot, David Coulthard, had announced he was quitting Formula One at the climax of the 2008 campaign. But Dario was committed to staying in the vocation which he loved. He was privileged to be in a situation where he could spend the summer enjoying an extended holiday with Ashley in Scotland, in addition to sailing boats and chewing the fat with his brother, Marino, and there were even suggestions that he could be ready to join his sibling in the American Le Mans series. He was also on friendly terms with the NASCAR owner, Richard Childress, who had spoken of fielding a fourth car in the near future. There was the further possibility that Ganassi might eventually dispense with the services of Reed Sorenson, whose performances had hardly been anything to write home about. But what became evident, amid the gossip, was that Dario still had the motoring bug and wasn't ready to consider any alternative life. 'I have lots of options and that is good to know, but I will have to look at them all before making a decision. Everything about the [NASCAR] move was hard, and when you sit back and realise that the team hasn't been competitive, it becomes even more difficult. It had definitely been a character-building season, and it took a while to sink in when Chip told me what was happening, but I have committed myself to seven more Nationwide races with the Ganassi team, because I really want to keep learning how to drive these cars.' Franchitti was speaking at the start of August, at the same time confirming that he was disinclined to contemplate a return to the IRL. 'I am just not convinced I want to race on the big ovals in an IndyCar again, because I thoroughly enjoyed my time there, but that is in the past and I don't see the point of going back to something in which I have already been the champion. Those tracks are a lot of fun with a stock car, but not as much with an IndyCar, and that should tell you something about my experiences in 2008.'

The message could scarcely have been more insistent. Namely, that although Franchitti had been blighted by all manner of travails since being paraded in front of the cameras by Ganassi, he was as resolute as ever in his pledge to crack the stock-car code if offered the opportunity. As his contemporary, Hornish Jnr, had declared, it was one hell of a puzzle to decipher, and there were no guarantees that he would ever enjoy the same mastery and control which had been his hallmarks in CART and the IRL. But he knew that the task was worth persisting with and that he couldn't merely slink away to a permanent holiday. What he could not have envisaged was the firmness with which the NASCAR door had been slammed shut.

12

Keeping It in the Family

Somewhere in the psyche of many great sports stars, there lurks a feeling of immortality: a belief that the normal rules of the ageing process do not apply to them and that they can engineer their path beyond the attentions of old Father Time. This perhaps explains why so many leading personalities have clung on to the remnants of their careers, where commonsense dictated that retirement was a wiser option. Some of the biggest luminaries in their pursuits – such as Michael Schumacher, Jackie Stewart, Pete Sampras and Annika Sorenstam – have bowed out at the proper time, with their lustre undiminished by the ticking of the clock. Yet there are others – people in the mould of Maradona, Lance Armstrong, Nigel Mansell and golf's Nicklaus/Palmer/Player triumvirate – who have seemed addicted to the limelight, and have been unable to glide gracefully away from centre stage without the move generating a major void in their lives. It is a defining moment in any human being's existence – the instant when he or she resolves to seek a fresh start and embark on a new challenge – but too often for comfort, the magnetic attraction of celebrity ensures that champions hang on long after their sell-by date.

At the age of 35, where did this leave Dario Franchitti? He had always possessed a young man's outlook and a boyish enthusiasm for everything connected with his vocation, but when Chip Ganassi closed down his NASCAR team at the start of July, 2008, it surely signalled, as Churchill almost said, if not the beginning of the end, then certainly the start of his departure from motor-sport, and marked the recognition that he was far closer to the conclusion than he was to the outset of his life in the fast lane.

At least he could derive comfort from the reaction of many of his fellow Sprint Cup competitors to the news of Ganassi's actions. 'I think that a couple of things happened. Dario is an accomplished race car driver and I think he could get the job done in NASCAR, but it was going to take time and the question is: how patient can people be?' declared Jeff Burton, a veteran of the stock–car beat, with a rich crop of prizes to his name. 'And at a time when we don't have a lot of new sponsors coming into our sport, it is hard to build a company that wants to be patient. People who are making any serious investment want to see success right away. So, I think that a lot of things stacked up against Dario, and it made it harder for him than if he would have been able to have success sooner. Unfortunately, Ganassi have been a little down too [a good point, which was often overlooked elsewhere], and they haven't been as good as you would have expected them to be.'

The Roush Fenway competitor, Greg Biffle, lent his voice to the debate, offering the opinion that it might have been a different story if Franchitti and his No 40 Dodge team had simply stuck at the bottom of the standings for month after month, without demonstrating that they were building up momentum, amidst the growing pains. 'It is really shocking for us to see a team shut down like that, and it is very tough [for those who lost their jobs],' said Biffle. 'You don't want to see that. I think Dario is a great driver and he has improved tremendously in NASCAR. He ran very well at Loudon and qualified decently, but I don't know, there was something going on. Their organisation has been having a tough time competition-wise lately and it is sad to see them without a sponsor and being forced into the position of having to shut down temporarily.'

These words signified that Franchitti's rivals had detected the chill wind of recession in what had happened to the Scot. If Ganassi – a man who was enjoying as much success in the IRL as his personnel were toiling in stock cars – couldn't make a success of his new venture, then what message did that send out to any would-be investors? 'I think it is certainly a wake-up call, you know, and it shows that any of us are vulnerable, because I never would have thought that they would have struggled getting sponsorship,' said the four-time NASCAR champion, Jeff Gordon. 'I'm sure that Chip Ganassi thought that they wouldn't struggle. They [the new team] probably didn't think that they would struggle on the race track as much as they have, especially on the road course. We can all be vulnerable and it just makes you appreciate what you have, be grateful for the sponsors you have, and it makes you work that much harder to stay competitive.'

As the weeks elapsed, it became evident that Franchitti's commitment to NASCAR was unlikely to secure him any prolonged tenure on the circuit. In which light, it was hardly surprising that, after meeting with Ganassi on a number of occasions, he began to consider a volte-face on his previous decision not to return to the Indy Racing League.

In some respects, this idea initially seemed destined for failure, not least because Dario himself had done such a convincing job of closing the door on the IRL, but racing drivers have to be ready to adapt to circumstances and few in the Stateside game were more attuned to the process than the experienced Scot. Naturally, there remained myriad reservations about how matters could have deteriorated so quickly since the bold, strident talk at the start of the season, but as Mike Brudenell of the *Detroit Free Press* told me, most of the blame for his NASCAR woes lay with Ganassi, not anybody else.

'How on earth did somebody of Franchitti's ability struggle so badly in stock-car racing? Ask Juan Pablo Montoya, who has also driven in the Sprint Cup, or Indy 500 champion Sam Hornish Jnr, who is having his problems at Penske Racing. Running up front, week in, week out, in NASCAR might appear easy if you are Jimmie Johnson or Kyle Busch, but, in truth, it is the hardest thing to do in racing. And that is if you are in a top team, which Ganassi hasn't been in a long time,' declared Brudenell, who was an accomplished enough performer in his own right to appreciate the differences. 'You need the team. You need the sponsors. You need an engine builder. You need a smart crew chief. You need time. You need information. And you don't just get there by being successful in another series, particularly in one which has few similarities to the Sprint Cup.

'Franchitti is one of the best open-wheel racers around, but he didn't arrive in NASCAR from the short tracks. He didn't drive in late models, he didn't drive super modifieds or sprint cars or midgets. He didn't race on quarter-mile and half-mile ovals. He didn't rub fenders at bull-rings or drive big, heavy cars with marginal brakes and slow reflexes. So he jumped in at the deep end when he moved from the IRL.' In short, it was a gamble which might have paid off, given the luxury of time, sponsorship and an owner with a blank cheque. But this certainly didn't apply in Dario's case. 'You are playing catch-up from the first day you turn up, and if you throw in another 43 very tough Cup drivers, it's an incredibly steep learning curve,' Brudenell told me at the start of September, 2008. 'I think that Franchitti, with a better team, might have made the grade in NASCAR. But at Ganassi, I am not sure whether he was ever comfortable in the Dodge [vehicle].'

Like many of the ice floes in Sarah Palin's Alaska, the issue could no longer be skated over. The switch to the stock-car domain had failed and the parties concerned needed to come up with a face-saving plan and do so quickly. In which circumstances, it was not particularly surprising when the news arrived on the afternoon of September 2 that Dario had agreed terms to rejoin the IRL for the 2009 campaign – on a multi-year deal - with Chip Ganassi's organisation, as a restructuring programme was implemented with admirable precision and synchronised timing, following the move to Panther Racing of the Englishman Dan Wheldon. At first glance, there was no disguising the fact that this constituted a rather embarrassing about-turn, but there again, sport is full of stubborn, obstinate people who refuse to change tack, despite the evidence in front of their own eyes. At least Franchitti and Ganassi had cleared the decks, accepted that a new direction was required, and prepared themselves for a damage limitation exercise.

'It is going to be very exciting to have Dario in one of our IndyCars [alongside his former rival, Scott Dixon], next year. I have always admired his competitive spirit when he raced against us and have really grown to see more of what he is about [as a person] this season while he raced in NASCAR,' said the ubiquitous Chip. 'When there was a possibility of an opening on our IndyCar team, the only person I thought about for the job was Dario. This is going to be a great move, both for Dario and the Target team.'

For his part, Franchitti was clearly relieved to have his

future plans verified, even though he couldn't quite disguise his view that he could have cut the mustard in the NASCAR sphere. 'Part of the reason that I signed with Ganassi last year was because of how many options Chip had at his disposal for a driver. You can do almost any form of racing that you want. With unification and the new [IndyCar series] schedule having more road and street course, it made me think about this more and more,' said Dario. 'I have really enjoyed this season in stock cars and have not completely closed that chapter on my professional career, but the opportunity that has arisen was just something which I could not pass up. I am really looking forward to getting behind the wheel of one of those Target cars and being a team-mate of Scott's, whom I know well. Target is a tremendous sponsor and they and Chip always give you everything that you need to win.'

None of these words could gloss over the reality that Dario's excursion into NASCAR had been one of the most difficult periods of his motoring life. And, regardless of the bonhomie between him and Ganassi, some sporting outlets viewed the announcement as proof that Franchitti should never have left the IRL in the first place. Marcus Simmons, who works for *Autosport* magazine, told me: 'This is an admission that he failed at NASCAR, isn't it? But I am actually pleased, because it is a big-name driver moving from NASCAR to IndyCar, rather than the other way around for a change.' These sentiments were widely reciprocated in the United States, where Mike Brudenell observed: 'It appears that Franchitti is home again, driving in 2009 for Target Chip Ganassi Racing. Perhaps Juan Montoya and some others should join him.'

Yet, despite his problems in this new environment, Franchitti was still able to celebrate the growing maturity of his young cousin, Paul Di Resta, who, in common with

Dario, has made a favourable impression in the DTM series and is already being tipped to follow Lewis Hamilton into the realm of Formula One. It is quite a connection the families have established over the years, and while Paul may be a different customer from Dario – he doesn't have the latter's slick PR sheen at the moment, for instance – the two West Lothian lads have formed an alliance, which is designed to ensure that the 22-year-old doesn't have to give up on his dreams, which he has cherished ever since the pint-sized Paul was pottering around with machinery before he had even gone to school.

'It just occurred naturally. Nobody ever put any pressure on me to get interested in cars, but I began playing around with them from the time I was knee-high to a grasshopper, and I can't remember a time when I wasn't champing at the bit to go faster and faster,' says Paul, his words eerily reminiscent of Dario at the same stage of his development. 'It must be something in the genes – both of our families have been obsessed with motor-sport all their lives – but I also think that we have recognised that you won't get anywhere if you are aiming in five or six different directions, so we have stuck together like glue. I don't want it to sound corny, but my dad [Louis] has been my rock, my inspiration, he has helped me along every step of the road, and I know that whatever happens in the future, the family ties will be unbreakable. I have heard that you have to be ruthless to succeed in motor-sport, but you do not have to sacrifice your decency in the process, and that lesson has been handed down from generation to generation. Ask my father – he is still as much in love with racing as he was when he was a boy. Ask Dario – he has shown me how you can climb up the ladder if you have the right attitude. And both these people have offered me a huge amount of encouragement and support.'

Louis, who watched Dario's gradual rise to fame, responds to questions with a rapid-fire delivery and once and he and Paul have sat down together, their conversation unfolds in the mould of verbal ping-pong, which is not really surprising, considering the amount of time each has spent in the other's company. 'Over the last few years, I have owned two vans, one has done 100,000 miles, the other 100,000 kilometres, so we have stacked up around 175,000 miles, journeying from Bathgate down to England and into Europe and going wherever we have to keep Paul's career on track,' says Louis, a relentlessly coiled spring of strong opinions and bold assertions. 'I guess that when you factor in the distances we have travelled to go to a load of different karting circuits, Paul and I have gone over a quarter of a million miles together, so nobody can accuse us of not being wholehearted about this and getting off our backsides and making it a reality . . .'

'But you can't do it any other way,' interjects Paul, whose pragmatism off the track is at odds with his ferocious pursuit of success on it. 'Motor-sport is a global business and there are hundreds of youngsters out there, making sacrifices and asking their parents for money, and striving to climb up the ladder, and you can't afford to wait for people to give you hand-outs. I guess it is a bit like a wanting to become a top footballer in the English Premiership. You are not going to attract the attention of the likes of Manchester United, Arsenal or Chelsea if you turn out for Bathgate Thistle every Saturday, are you?'

This was the same philosophy espoused by Franchitti as he pondered his options, whilst competing on the DTM circuit. Basically, he could attempt to keep hanging on by his fingernails, scraping by on a shoe string budget, or he could be proactive, grab the opportunity offered to him by Mercedes and venture to the Big Country with equally lofty aspirations. Certainly, Dario, who collected the

McLaren/Autosport Young Driver prize in 1992, a little matter of 13 years before Di Resta followed in his footsteps, has no doubts over the prowess of his youthful compatriot and has emerged as a secondary father figure to Louis. ('I'm okay with arranging meetings and settling the basics, but when it comes to contracts and legal negotiations, I leave all that stuff to Dario,' says Louis). And, despite being based thousands of miles away, Franchitti is unperturbed by the experience of becoming enmeshed in transatlantic bonding with his protégé. 'I am tremendously excited about Paul and the sky is the limit for him, because getting involved with Mercedes, who have one of the best development programmes in the business, is exactly where he needs to be,' says Dario. 'If he stays level-headed, and continues to do what he has been doing every year he has been racing, he can achieve anything he desires. He might make it in the States, he might do it in F1 or in sports cars, like Allan McNish. That depends on what avenues open up for him. But talent-wise, it is simply not an issue. He has all the ingredients required to do well at the highest level, I am in regular contact with him, and I do not believe there is anybody among the young contenders anywhere [within the world of motor-sport] who is hungrier or more focused than Paul.'

In common with Dario, whose CV now boasts honours in several different spheres of racing, Di Resta hails from the no-bull school of sport, where he speaks his mind, accepts that danger is an inherent part of the business, and refuses to get drawn into slagging off opponents or being distracted by issues outwith his vocation. As somebody who has already rubbed shoulders with David Coulthard, Jenson Button, Mika Hakkinen, Ralf Schumacher and the majority of modern F1 luminaries, Di Resta is no more inclined to starry-eyed nonsense than Dario was when he was growing up, flitting between Bathgate, Whitburn, Inverness, Ingliston and

Larkhall, oblivious to the risks involved in his ambitions. 'I was with Dario about ten minutes before he was involved in a serious biking accident [in 2003], and his career was in jeopardy for a period, but it has never remotely entered my mind that the same thing could happen to me,' says Paul. 'In the bigger picture, you accept that good and bad things happen and that sometimes life isn't fair, but if you were to allow your life to be ruled by fear, you would never get out of bed in the morning. Dario lost his best friend in an IndyCar race in 1999, and that was terrible. But it didn't stop him from climbing back into the car and pushing himself to the limit a few months later and I have the same attitude. If you love something, the risk element doesn't really come into it.'

Whenever the Franchittis and Di Restas convene for a family meal, it is inevitable that motoring will enter the conversation at some point and invariably sooner rather than later. After all, Dario's brother, Marino, has carved out an excellent reputation on the American Le mans circuit, without making a song and dance about his achievements, whilst the likes of Louis' niece, Bianca, drove karts for a few months, Paul's younger brother, Stefan, was drawn to karts like a cobra to a mongoose, and they collectively revel in the genealogy and the Scottish and Italian traits which have shaped and moulded them.

This brings us back, almost to the place where we began, in the rough and ready milieu of Bathgate at the weekly Friday market. In the midst of visiting the community in 2005, following on from Dario Franchitti's Indy 500 triumph, I sought out a range of views on his achievement from some of the locals and had been offered a few comments along the lines of 'That's great,' 'That's brilliant, man.' Or 'I couldn't give a xxxx, mate.' One old worthy, who must have been around 80 and who seemed to have digested every newspaper clipping about Scottish motor racing from the year dot, then spent the best part of the next hour, regaling me with his memories of the old racing days and how the new generation didn't realise how fortunate they were. (I didn't manage to get a word in edgeways, which was probably just as well, or I would still be talking to the fellow.)

However, once I had escaped his clutches, the most articulate observation came from a spiky-haired young man, who was waiting for the hourly train service from Bathgate into Newcraighall in Edinburgh. 'I suppose that it's nice to be in the newspapers for something other than a murder or a factory shutting down, because West Lothian needs all the good news it can find, but while I am very pleased for Dario and he has been a great ambassador for the area, let's be honest here. This isnae Hollywood.'

He was, of course, correct, both in a geographical sense, and in the wider fact that Dario has moved into a different world from the one in which he grew up. And yet, for all that he now has a film actress wife, enough money to ensure that he never needs to work another day in his life unless he feels like it, and a range of gadgets, accessories, private vehicles and property which are beyond the comprehension of the majority of those who reside in West Lothian, Franchitti's attitude towards his job, towards tackling and facing up to challenges, and his refusal to give up the ghost, represent the best qualities from the region which has recently paid tribute to one of their most famous sons, even before his exploits were applauded by the Scottish Government. It would be even better if the country which boasts the likes of Clark, Stewart, Coulthard, McRae, McNish and Franchitti actually invested in the process of assisting future champions – as Sir Jackie has long advocated – but there again, the likes of Dario have generally prevailed in spite of, not because of, the sports funding in their homeland.

In short, it would be unwise to dismiss Franchitti's ambitions to become a champion again in the Indy Racing League, just as it would be foolish to write off Paul Di Resta's desire to meet and beat the saintly Lewis Hamilton at some stage in the future of Formula One. These people are brave, they are bloody-minded, they lack neither self-belief, nor will they shirk from adversity, nor ignore the consequences of their actions, however distressing they may be in some cases. Ultimately, Whitburn and the surrounding communities have changed dramatically from the days in the 1970s when the sound of the siren going off during the night used to signify that some poor bugger had been killed or suffered a grievous injury within the bowels of Polkemmet Colliery and that the town would be in mourning within the next two or three days as he was laid to rest. We should be glad that such tragedies are now consigned to the past throughout Scotland, but we should also appreciate that the values which used to thrive in these places still beat today, even if successive governments have done their best to destroy such concepts as families and society pulling together for one another in a common cause, except, or so it seems, when tragedy strikes.

All of which is a way of stating that Dario Franchitti might have enjoyed the bulk of his success in America and he has recently been earning vast sums of money in an arcane activity – if you doubt this, then just ask the person next to you to explain what the acronym, NASCAR, stands for! But he has never deserted his homeland, nor been interested in becoming a tax exile, unlike some of his motoring contemporaries. It may be the case that he is not in the same class as a Michael Schumacher or Ayrton Senna – the two greatest drivers of the last 30 years – but, given the singular fashion in which he has earned a quiet greatness, whether at home or abroad, we should applaud this fellow and revel in his talents, his devotion to sport, and commitment to passing on the torch to Paul.

It used to be that West Lothian had pits. Now, the area is unearthing a conveyor belt of talent who are basking in the paddock as well. In anybody's language, whether it be Scottish or Italian, that has to be a source of encouragement and inspiration.

After all, if 2008 has proved a source of frustration and occasional angst to Franchitti, he has shown repeatedly throughout his career that he possesses the capacity to transform adversity to advantage. On his return to the Indy Racing League, he will be doubly motivated, both as a consequence of his NASCAR travails and because it is one thing to win a major title, but another thing entirely to claim that prize twice. Dario accepts that it won't be easy and that he will be up against one of the best competitors in the business in his Ganassi colleague, Dixon, but he is excited at the prospect of returning to the domain where he strolled out of the shadows and became a household name in America.

'The trepidation is that you want to make sure you can still do the job. You believe that you can do it, but until you can see it, there is always that nagging doubt. I want to be as good as or better than when I left,' said Franchitti, who still retains a burning ambition to excel on the stock-car stage. 'It was all about the challenge to do that. And, my God, was it a challenge. If I had to do it again, I would probably try and get a bit more testing and a bit more build-up before getting in there. It was one of those deals where I felt this year that everything that could go wrong did go wrong. But, looking back, I wouldn't change anything. I would make the same choice again [to join NASCAR]. I got to experience something which was completely different and perhaps I will do so again in the future. Who knows? But this is definitely a positive way for me to go into next year.'

The words reflect Franchitti's philosophy and the tenets which have guided him through his serried career. He doesn't have anything left to prove to those in his slipstream, but although one suspects that Dario could comfortably carve out a niche as a commentator on motor-sport or even become involved in the establishment of a new team, he is a youthful 35, not the kind of old fogey who idles away the hours in *recherché du temps perdu*. In January this year, for instance, he had been sitting having his usual breakfast cereal at his and Ashley's residence in Nashville when a stalker broke into the couple's home and Dario subsequently pursued the intruder in the sort of car chase which might have been lifted from an episode of *Miami Vice*. Such was the pandemonium in the ensuing 20 or 30 seconds that the Scot didn't have time to put his trousers on before pursuing the trespasser, but there was no denying the instinctive bravery which he exhibited as the prelude to his quarry being caught in a police road block. 'When they came up to me, I realised that I was still in my boxer shorts and I couldn't leave the car,' was his nonchalant response to media inquiries over what many people would have regarded as a shocking incident. 'I don't think that he [the stalker] wanted to meet me. It was Ashley he wanted to see.'

After these kind of matters off the track, one imagines that picking up the reins anew in the IRL in 2009 will be a breeze by comparison.

Ultimately, his qualities were forged from the place where he originated. Almost nothing fazes Franchitti. But there again, they don't call it Wild West Lothian for nothing!

INDEX